Love Slaves

D1125623

Love Slaves

How to End
Your Addiction
to Another
Person

Dr. Bernard Green

BOB ADAMS, INC.
Holbrook, Massachusetts

Published by Bob Adams, Inc.
260 Center Street, Holbrook, MA 02343

ISBN: 1-55850-290-4

Printed in the United States of America

A   B   C   D   E   F   G   H   I   J

Library of Congress Cataloging-in-Publication Data
Green, Bernard, 1934-
    Love slaves : how to end your addiction to another person.
    p.   cm.
    Includes index.
    ISBN 1-55850-290-4 : $8.95
    1. Relationship addiction. I. Title.
    RC552.R44G74   1993
    616.85'227   93-34577
                                                        CIP

The names used in case studies appearing in this book are not the names of actual
persons. These names are fictitious.

COVER DESIGN: Marshall Henrichs

This book is available at quantity discounts for bulk purchases.
For information, call 1-800-872-5627.

Dedicated to Judith,
whose love helped me enjoy the present,
and to Tyler, my son,
whose love helped me let go of the past
and to Ted,
who made all this happen,
thank you.

Table of Contents

I would like to acknowledge:

Daphne Davis
Hyde School
Pir Vilyat Khan
Kate Layzer
Blair C. Marshall
Claiborne T. Marshall
Ted Schwarz
Bill Thompson
Brandon Toropov

. . . and all those who struggle to love and be loved.

Chapter 1

What Is a Love Slave?

It was the relationship made in heaven. Amy knew that—had known it since she and Rick first fell in love. He sent her flowers at the advertising agency where she worked in the art department. He invited himself to dinner at her apartment several weeks after they first began dating, but rather than have her cook, he brought the ingredients and prepared the meal himself. His skills weren't the greatest, but he managed to produce a meal even Julia Child would have found pleasant. Later, over glasses of brandy, he confessed that he had practiced the dinner for two weeks, and that his refrigerator was filled with leftovers from his early failures. He had just wanted to impress her, he said. To make her happy.

Marriage was inevitable. Amy and her friends knew she'd be crazy if she let Rick slip away. He was totally devoted to her; respectful; loving. He wanted only the best for her, even if that meant subverting his goals for hers. He made it clear that, though he was in a management program in a bank, if she ever needed to move for her career, he'd gladly start over.

The marriage was more exciting than the courtship. They worked their schedules so they could meet for lunch each day at a small restaurant halfway between her job and his. They prepared meals together. They cleaned together. They went to movies and concerts. They were so inseparable that, on their sixth-month anniversary, their friends jokingly gave them a pair of toy plastic handcuffs because they seemed so closely joined.

It was in the early fall that something began changing. Amy was promoted, and with the raise came greater responsibilities. When the agency began aggressively seeking new business, she became part of a team that not only serviced existing clients but prepared support materials for pitch meetings by the account executives. She explained to Rick that she needed more time and wanted to cut back on their lunches. She felt that if she could eat at her drawing board, she could get most of the extra work done and have the majority of her evenings and weekends free.

Rick agreed to cut back, but after the first week, he began calling her on the telephone during the time they normally had lunch. He said he was lonely. He said he missed her. He said he loved her. And always he apologized for interrupting. Some of her friends thought it was sweet. Others wondered if he was checking up on her.

The changes in the relationship were subtle at first. Rick asked about the male members of the creative team. Were they gay or straight? Were they married or single? If they were married, did they cheat on their wives? If they were single, were they in committed relationships or constantly on the make?

When Amy was sent out of town for some special training on a new computer graphics program the agency was planning to use, Rick "surprised" her by showing up at the hotel. He was seated in the lobby, reading a book and waiting for her to appear. He said the concierge had recommended an expensive French restaurant in the area that had an excellent reputation. He had made reservations, if she was free.

Amy was both pleased and disappointed. She told him she wished he had talked with her first before flying out. She had more classes to take in the morning and needed to study the manuals she had been given, along with her notes. She had planned to order room service and work until she was too tired to do anything but go to sleep. The material was so involved, she wanted to be certain she had as many questions answered as possible before the course was over.

Rick was understanding, of course. The reservations could be canceled. He would stay in the room with her, reading. That was all he wanted, really. Just to be with her. Unless she had planned to study with one of the men who had gone to the training with her. If that was her plan, then he'd stay in the lobby. He didn't want to intrude. He just wanted her to be happy. He just wanted her to be successful. And he certainly trusted her. He didn't think she'd be using the time she thought they would be apart to have an affair.

Although Amy said nothing that night, after they returned home late Sunday, she began worrying about her relationship with Rick. It wasn't that he was falling out of love with her. If anything he had become more intensely devoted to her, aggressive in their lovemaking, self-sacrificing, always trying to be certain she was happy. It was just that he seemed almost too devoted to her, if such a situation was possible. He seemed to be subverting his own life, his own desires, for hers. By the time they had been married two years, Amy realized she knew little more about her husband than she had when she married him. He claimed that her interests were his interests, her friends were his friends, her taste in art, music, theater, and literature matched his exactly.

Yet she knew that wasn't true. He had loved classic rock music when she first met him, while she was an early jazz buff. He delighted in action-adventure paperbacks, calling it escapist fiction to relieve the tensions of the banking world. She read Danielle Steele, Mary Higgins Clark, and Sidney Sheldon. He had a modest collection of American coins, a hobby she found boring, preferring to collect old advertising posters.

Now he read what she read, though she knew he found it uninteresting. He sold his record and tape collection, using the money to buy records, tapes, and CDs of jazz recordings Amy had not yet acquired. And the coins had been placed in a safe-deposit box at his bank, never to be mentioned again, while their walls were filled with framed advertising art.

Amy had not wanted a clone of herself. She wanted a man who was independent, vibrant, interesting as much because of his differences as because of what they shared. She wanted each to help the other grow, and while she delighted in his devotion, she was also finding it smothering. His effort to exactly match what she did, what she read, even what she thought about politics, religion, and the concerns of the day made him less desirable. The plastic handcuffs they had placed on the wall over the bed had once symbolized loving unity. Now she saw them as symbolizing bondage, that she was his prisoner.

Yet how do you explain to someone totally devoted that you no longer love him? How do you tell a man who so adores you that he would happily give up his job and sit with you twenty-four hours a day that you want less ardor? How do you explain to a man who constantly worries about your having an affair that you want more time to yourself? How do you say that a little more distance would rekindle love, when he sees separation as proof of infidelity? What do you say to a man who truly means it when he tells you, "Treat me as your 'love slave' and I will devote my life to making you happy"?

Eventually there was a divorce, of course. There had to be. Amy was uncertain from what she was running, but she knew that continuing with Rick was unhealthy for both of them.

———————————

The French call them "love slaves." American therapists talk of obsessive love. Whatever the term, they are the men and women who cannot let go in a relationship. They are often highly intelligent, hard working, and intensely caring. They seldom use drugs or drink to excess, and they have no intention of cheating on a lover or spouse. Yet their devotion is not based on the relationship they are experiencing. It evolves from long suppressed, unfulfilled needs from childhood.

Love slaves have a consistency to their pasts. Their childhoods were lacking in the nurturing they needed, often through no one's fault. Some were children who lost the full-time presence of one of their parents through divorce, separation, or death. Others had a parent or parents who were struggling so hard to make ends meet that the child was left on his or her own longer than was emotionally healthy. Sometimes there was deliberate emotional neglect. Other times the child simply had needs greater than circumstances allow a devoted parent to fulfill. Whatever the case, the man or woman coming from such a background subconsciously feels a failure. If only he or she had behaved differently, the parent(s) would have given more attention, been more nurturing. Or so the thought process goes.

Adults raised with such inadvertent or deliberate neglect need to understand the reality of their early life. Some seek counseling. Others simply reflect on their childhoods with the understanding that comes from maturity. And both types heal, recognizing that they were victims of circumstances that had nothing to do with them. They see that it was their parents who had problems, that they were always worthy of love, that circumstances for their mothers and fathers created the conditions in which they were raised. They may forgive their parents, or they may simply accept that they cannot go back and correct what was a bad situation. They move forward into healthy relationships, trying not to make the same mistakes with their own families.

But some men and women coming from such backgrounds do

not come to an understanding of their pasts or how that past colors their present perceptions. They are the individuals who project their fantasies and their needs onto the person with whom they are having a relationship. They do not truly come to know their lovers or spouses. But they convince themselves that unless they can sustain a relationship, even if it proves to be the wrong one, they will continue to be the "failures" they were in childhood. Thus they will do anything to keep their partner, constantly fearing loss, and often demeaning themselves in the process. Certainly that was the problem for Sheila.

————————————

Sheila's story was different from Amy's. She was a stunningly beautiful woman, as intelligent and personable as she was good-looking. She worked her way through one of the Ivy League colleges by modeling for catalogs and some of the smaller cosmetics companies. She also got into broadcasting, her lilting voice considered perfect for voice-overs and commercials. By the time she was involved with Henry, she was a successful freelance actress, model, and part-time radio personality. There was talk of a cable television show, which, if popular, would be syndicated. She was earning a good living and seemed on the brink of national success.

Henry was as handsome as Sheila was beautiful, but where Sheila had depth, Henry was all flash without substance. He was a high-paid publishing executive through inheritance rather than skill, and even his father had no illusions. He made certain that a hand-picked staff of competent experts made all the decisions about running the company. Henry was given a plush office, a multi-line telephone, membership in a country club, and other perks—but his actual responsibilities were negligible.

Henry also liked women—young women, older women, short women and tall women. His idea of monogamy was to be with the same woman through the entire weekend. And since the vast majority of weekends were devoted to Sheila, it was several weeks into the relationship, after Sheila had fallen in love with Henry and thought he loved her, that she discovered how he spent his weekdays.

The crisis occurred in one of New York's nicest restaurants, Tavern on the Green. She was being feted by the producer of the planned cable television show, who wanted to sign her to a long-term contract in case her success proved as great as everyone hoped. Henry was taking a long lunch hour, attempting to get a photographer's representative he had met drunk and mellow enough to stop by an area hotel for some early-afternoon recreation. It was obvious by the way he was touching her, joking with her, and subtly refilling her glass with wine just what he had in mind.

Henry turned pale when he saw Sheila as she walked past him on the way to the ladies' room. She, on the other hand, remained impassive, as though not seeing him, determined to put her horror out of her mind until she was alone.

There were the usual recriminations, of course. Henry tried to claim it was a more innocent lunch than it looked. He tried to claim she was a distant cousin, a long-lost friend, an old college sweetheart with whom he was reliving old times but who no longer meant anything intimate to him. The excuses were so varied that Sheila hired a private investigator, who confirmed her worst fears. Henry was a philanderer who seemed to separate sex and love, if, indeed, he had ever loved her at all. She confronted Henry with the evidence, and naturally he had no excuse. Of course he would never "darken her doorstep again," although what had happened would not interfere with any business relationship she might have with one of his father's companies. They both knew it was all over between them.

And yet it was less than a week after the break-up that Sheila found herself waiting outside Henry's office building at noon, watching to see when he left. He had no fixed pattern for eating, leaving any time between 12:00 and 1:00 p.m. for some reason. She wanted to be certain that she did not miss him.

Soon Sheila found herself checking on Henry more and more. She went to his apartment. She went to the restaurants and night spots where they had gone together. She went to the locations the private investigator had noted in his report. Sometimes she telephoned him at odd hours, listening to whomever answered the telephone and then hanging up without saying anything. She was frequently asked for dates by men she knew she could trust, men who respected and desired her for her abilities, yet she turned them all down. She was obsessed with Henry, obsessed with the fantasy of getting him back, of restoring the love she knew they had never shared. Her memory became selective, with only the good times lingering in her thoughts. She felt she dared not seek a new relationship because then she would be the one who was unfaithful. Then she would be the one who was wrong.

Henry did not change, of course. He treated women as he had always done. If he became cautious, it was in selecting those who would not make demands of commitment on him. Sheila had been a mistake.

Eventually Henry became aware of some of Sheila's actions. Just as they had accidentally encountered one another at the Tavern on the Green, so there were instances when they inadvertently met when she was following him. Always she mumbled some sort of excuse, then fled from the location. And always he was puzzled by what was taking place. He even tried calling her once, thinking she still loved him, wanted him, might give him a delightful time in bed much as she had in the past. Yet when he reached her, she was all anger and hate. She despised him, his lifestyle, and the idea that he might still be trying to use her. Her verbal attack was so great that her seeming obsession with him made no sense. He never knew that Sheila was as confused by her own actions as he was.

Sheila was as much of a "love slave" as Rick had been. But where Rick had been devoted to what seemed, at first, to be a perfect relationship, Sheila was obsessed with a man who was worthless as a partner by anyone's standards. Yet she refused even to consider changing her patterns until friends convinced her that she needed counseling. By the time she came to my office, she had not been involved with Henry for almost three years, though she continued to find excuses for trying to be where she might encounter him.

Our culture tends to romanticize obsessive love—popular culture especially. Twentieth-century musical theater, motion pictures, rock music lyrics, and even some contemporary rap songs endlessly glorify the idea of total devotion. There is nothing more perfect than a relationship where the pleasures and pain of the real world disappear in a man's and a woman's rapture with one another. The ideal seems to be commitment that transcends all other involvements, all other realities of life.

"Night and day, you are the one . . ."

"Totally devoted to you . . ."

"I can't give you anything but love . . ."
"I want to get you on a slow boat to China, all to myself alone . . ."
"Till the end of time . . ."
"I've got you deep in the heart of me . . ."
"Forever . . ."

The lyrics of thousands of love songs focus on the idea of obsessive love, of each lover being a "love slave" to the other. Many of the country western "cheatin' heart" songs, as well as many blues lyrics, reflect the pain of a devoted lover who can never relate to anyone but the love object who has done the spurning. One person is committed "forever." The other person has failed to understand what a wonderful opportunity he or she is shattering.

Movies may reflect the pain of divorce, but true happiness comes when the woman finds Mr. Right or the man finds Ms. Right, and the audience knows they will never part. After all, don't fairy tales frequently end with the words, "And they lived happily ever after"? Real life has Britain's Royal Family falling apart through neglect, emotional stiffness, and all-too-public affairs. But if the House of Windsor were the fairy-tale House of Charming, then Diana would have been Cinderella, and Prince Charles would have been the Prince Charming with whom "ever after" is always blissful. Unfortunately, love slaves tend to involve themselves with the Windsors, then try to create the world of the Charmings.

Romance novels frequently have as a theme the idea of the strong woman holding a man in disdain for his casualness towards others. The two clash, and she refuses to be just another of his brief affairs. By the end of the book, he has become so overwhelmingly in love with her that he confesses his weaknesses and shows her that he has changed. They go off into the sunset, the reader knowing once again that he is committed to her "forever."

I was once a believer in the ideal of total devotion between partners. As happens so often, my first marriage was the victim of partners who were simply too young, too unrealistic about life, and burdened by mutual expectations neither of us could fulfill for each other. During the period of emotional pain that followed the divorce, I came to know people who were in an obsessive relationship. Sometimes the man was obsessed with the woman, sometimes the woman with the man, and sometimes each was obsessed with the other. To have someone so in love with you that they would be your love slave, doing everything possible to keep you happy, seemed wonderful.

This was not a sex fantasy. Although the couples I knew seemed to have a mutually enjoyable and supportive sex life, the act of being a love slave did not relate to the bedroom. Instead it was the complete sublimation of personal interests, goals, and activities whenever they might interfere with what they thought was the other person's happiness. The man's joy came from making the woman happy. The woman's joy came from making the man happy. The relationships involved every aspect of life, from work to hobbies, recreation, home, and family.

Over time, though, what had seemed perfect began to look troubled. Humans are social creatures who live best in community. In the extreme, you have the isolated extended families of communes so popular in the 1960s. More typical are the social lives we create to handle different aspects of our existence. One world involves our coworkers. Other worlds involve the members of a social club, bowling team, religious group, hobby organization—even the regulars at a coffee shop, bar, or restaurant. The more we narrow our involvements, the more stressful our lives, according to many studies related to physical and emotional health. While a loving, nurturing relationship is important for everyone, the totally devoted couples I knew seemed to withdraw from all others. They became emotional hermits together, severing critical relationships for the sake of "my one and only."

Then I noticed the constant tension of the obsessive lovers, a tension that came from jealousy. Each partner was certain that the other could not be loving him or her as much as the love that was given. A romantic weekend getaway could be ruined when he was certain she was making eyes at the hotel bellman and she accused him of being too interested in the restaurant waitress. If one went to the gift shop to get a newspaper, the other might wonder whom he or she was meeting.

Jealousy, insecurity, and outrageous fantasy grew like a cancer until it began to destroy the body of the relationship. Eventually each partner seemed to feel a love/hate attitude toward the other. Yet frequently they were unable to make a break, certain they could not live without each other.

When just one was the obsessively committed love slave, divorce was common, although the love slave would not accept the legalities. He or she would be trying desperately to find a way to restore a relationship everyone else could see was over. It was like a small child who, when faced with parents separating from one another, becomes certain that he or she has only to change to different behavior and everything will be right again. "If I clean up my room, will you stay together?" "If I eat all my peas, will you stay together?" "If I go to bed on time . . . ?"

For many years we therapists failed to recognize how many people suffer from obsessive love. We had not developed ways to analyze the problem. We did not see the lives that were being seriously hurt, the relationships shattered. We failed to recognize the pain, and we certainly did not know how to heal what amounts to an addiction to a fantasy focused on another person.

Often we chose language that caused people to deny or overlook the condition. A man might derisively be called "henpecked" or worse. A woman would either be put down as "old-fashioned" and out of step with contemporary society, or she would be lauded for following "traditional values." Yet the truth was not that the actions of the love slave were necessarily wrong. The problem was with the person's attitude.

Many men treasure their wives' unique abilities, their love for their jobs, their leadership in business or politics, or the happiness they derive from working in an area where the man's opportunities are limited. Child-raising chores are either taken over by the man or willingly shared. Compromises are constantly being worked out. Such men delight in what they sense to be a partnership requiring give and take. They know that the acceptance of minor frustrations also makes them open to greater pleasure than they ever thought possible.

Likewise, many women willingly put their spouse's career ahead of their own, often taking great pride in their ability to find work wherever they move. They like the flexibility of exploring such options as raising the children with or without a part-time job, of being periodically reeducated in new fields or in new business technology, of being an entrepreneur, of starting a business at home. New challenges are exciting, and they may wonder how their husbands are able to survive emotionally knowing they may hold the same job for forty or fifty years.

The love slave is different. He or she is totally obsessed with the relationship. No negative change, even one that is for the best, can be tolerated. The love slave becomes a walking doormat for the other, often causing the emotionally healthy party to lose respect. The love slave refuses to accept the reality of the other person, clinging to a fantasy that should be allowed to die. The love slave experiences constant anxiety, unable to be objective about the other person. And because their actions seem to others to be positive, no one—not friends, not co-workers, not even family members—recognize there is a problem.

Yet being a love slave is one of the most common problems faced by men and women in this country, made worse by the proliferation of deadly sexually transmitted diseases. It is sometimes perceived as easier to stay in a bad relationship where you are seemingly appreciated than to seek a healthy one and risk all the dangers of contemporary dating—even though neither love slave nor tolerating the obsessive lover brings anything but grief and frustration.

Are you a love slave? Do you find yourself staying in a relationship long after you know it is over? Do you find yourself wanting someone you know is no good for you? Are you unable to heal when someone you loved has not only broken off with you but is now committedly involved with another?

Whatever the case, this book will take you through the process needed to overcome such obsessive love and lead a normal, happy, productive, and enjoyable life. You will learn to enjoy a healthy, enriching, freeing, loving relationship.

In chapter 3 you will find a test I have given many times to help people like you understand their circumstances. Take it, being honest about yourself and about your loved one. Then, when you score it, you will know whether you have crossed over the boundaries of normal relationships into the world of the obsessive lover.

Chapter 2

Love–What Is It?

Researchers believe that romantic love was made possible when humans first started walking erect. There was physical attraction prior to that time, but it is believed that only when we were standing, able to observe each other completely, did romantic bonding occur. Certainly humans are among the few creatures in nature who naturally pair off as lovers for a prolonged period of time. And one of the reasons we form these bonds is chemical in nature. In fact, in its purest form, all romantic love is a form of healthy addiction. Through body chemistry changes, we are intensely linked for what, in nature, is an extensive interval of our lives.

The Chemistry of Love

Numerous physiological, psychological, and sensual experiences combine to link us with one partner and not another. Sometimes these are the smells of memory. One woman remembers a loving father whose body smelled of cigar smoke and whose breath smelled of beer. Arriving home from work, having first stopped for a quick drink at the neighborhood bar, he would burst through the door, calling his infant daughter's name, and take her in his arms, kissing her tiny face. His love was evident, overwhelming in a positive way, and the family bonding was strong. Though her father may have died when she was still a young woman, the subconscious memories result in the aroma of his brand of tobacco smoke being a major factor in her first strong attraction to a new man in her life.

By contrast, a woman whose father had similar pastimes but was intensely abusive to both the child and his wife would make very different associations with the same sensual experiences. She might encounter two men, each with similar backgrounds, education, and personalities, both of whom were perfect matches for her wants and needs. Yet if one of the men were a casual smoker and drinker and the other rarely smelled of tobacco or alcohol, she would be extremely uncomfortable with the former. Although perfect in every way, she would probably see him as slightly sinister, as having a dark side she fears encountering. The other man, seemingly identical to the casual eye, would be viewed as a uniquely perfect mate. This is why superficial characteristics such as baldness, weight, facial hair, height, aftershave or cologne, and even someone's name can result in a strong emotional response.

Styles of clothing, perfume, even certain foods affect how we perceive a potential lover. Growing up in a loving family environment where the kitchen always smelled of certain spices and seasonings means that such smells will give you a feeling of security as an adult. A woman who was raised in a nurturing environment where her mother was perpetually cooking spaghetti sauce was attracted to a man who owned an Italian restaurant. They eventually worked together, and she told me that each time she entered the big, noisy, commercial kitchen of their successful business, her mind transported her back to childhood. She felt warm and comfortable, knowing that whatever crisis she and her husband faced, somehow it would always work out for the best.

Likewise, another woman of my acquaintance was raised in a home where her parents were constantly fighting. The arguments inevitably occurred around dinner time, and since her father was originally from Mexico City, dinner was usually some kind of Mexican food. When this woman began dating a man from her office who seemed so perfect at first that she was certain she would marry him, she suddenly soured on the relationship the first night he told her how much he loved Mexican cooking. She feared that, somehow, he might turn into her father, and she was terrified of ending up with a marriage like the one her mother endured. She knew it was irrational, yet the relationship between certain odors and early childhood experience was too great in her mind to forget.

A man may react to perfume, breast size, make-up, hair style, or some other characteristic. He may be intimately drawn to a woman when her body is adorned with one fragrance and repelled by the same woman when, all else being equal, she is wearing a different fragrance.

Once a couple decides that they may be right for each other, new chemicals take over. The first is phenylethylamine. Although difficult to pronounce, it is easy to see the results of its production within the body. The person in love walks around smiling much of the time and may be oblivious to what is going on in the world at large. You've seen it: she gets on the freeway and drives three or four exits past where she wanted to go because she wasn't paying attention. Or trips over construction equipment because he was blissfully unaware of quite obvious warning signs. Or starts to walk into traffic because, although she looks at the street lights, the fact that the red is for her does not register. Then there's the guy in your office with the slightly loony, lopsided grin, oblivious to everyone he passes.

The chemistry that is created while one is in the throes of new love can make the lover look like a junkie experiencing a rush. This is because phenylethylamine is an amphetamine produced by the body. Falling in love so overloads the system that the lover is literally intoxicated. It is believed that the neurotransmitters norepinephrine and dopamine are also produced at the same time, although in lesser quantities. Narcotics addicts pay hundreds or thousands of dollars to buy enough drugs to try to achieve the same "high" that is naturally experienced by a person in love!

This is why love alters our moods for a period of time no matter what else is taking place with our bodies. I have had patients who were severely depressed from allergies, medical conditions, and emotional problems related to their past, all of whom have felt better for a time when they fell in love. It does not mean they are healed for the long term. The medical problems do not disappear. Unresolved past traumas still require counseling, although sometimes the person experiencing the first chemical reaction to new love does not understand this. "I just needed to fall in love again," such patients tell me, and for a while, they do feel much better. However, the intense manufacture of phenylethylamine is not continued throughout your life. It lasts for three or four years, at best, and then stops. Someone with depression may return to having to deal with the cause of that depression sooner than he or she expects.

Why is the chemical released for only a few years? No one knows, but some anthropologists feel that the four-year jolt is related to the way human babies develop. During the first four years of life, a child needs a great deal of attention in order to survive. A single parent is forced to take responsibility for all the needs of survival, from food gathering and preparation to the construction of shelter, manufacture of clothing, and protection of the young from predators. When a man and woman work together during those first four years, the child can get more attention, and life is easier. The child is also less likely to get seriously hurt, assuring the continuation of human existence.

Chemistry may also explain why some couples who have lived together for two or three years claim that "marriage ruins a good relationship." They don't realize that they are at the natural end of their initial amphetamine production. The drug that kept them so intensely involved with each other has worn off. At this time, one of two situations will occur in a healthy relationship. The first is that the couple will drift apart. They have become addicted to the high, which they now see as more likely to come from someone else. Perhaps a flirtation takes place. Perhaps there is touching, kissing, and just enough activity, short of intercourse with someone else, to bring on a new phenylethylamine rush. The person decides that he or she no longer loves the person who was Mr. or Ms. Right for so many months. This new person is the fresh love, and the process starts all over again.

More mature couples stay together, trying to understand what happened. Why is the intense passion fading away? And what can they do about it?

Now they try experiences other than intense sexual intercourse. They may talk more; spend time together exploring shared interests. They may hold hands, kiss, and cuddle. They try to be close in ways that were previously secondary, and they are biologically rewarded with the release of two new chemicals.

One is endorphin, a natural tranquilizer. This is the same chemical long-distance runners generate when they "hit the wall." For the runner this means that, after an intense struggle and near exhaustion, she suddenly feels exhilarated. She gets what she thinks of as her "second wind" and can go for many more miles in comfort. In reality she is simply releasing natural tranquilizers, the same tranquilizer that is released during the second stage of an intimate relationship.

In addition to the endorphins, the pituitary gland gives off oxytocin, which results in a feeling of well-being. Unlike the tranquilizing endorphin, oxytocin causes a person to seek the same experience again, with the result that intimacy becomes so comforting, you want to be with the person in a similar manner over and over. If you take the time to talk, to hold one another, to be close while relaxing, you will repeatedly seek the same sensation, constantly strengthening the bond despite the reduction of amphetamines. On the other hand, if you stop seeking such quiet closeness, eventually the lack of amphetamines and the failure to produce endorphins and oxytocin regularly will cause emotional estrangement. Then, if you let yourself seek other companionship, the return of phenylethylamine may cause you to want to commit adultery and/or get a divorce.

Loving intimacy, with or without intensely passionate sex, keeps the relationship to another person strong. A lack of such intimacy causes estrangement, separation, and/or divorce approximately four years after you are first together.

All of this means that love provides a safe, natural high that is intensely addicting. The secret to a happy, long-term committed relationship is stimulating chemistry several times a week through quiet, casual touch, sex, or any other activity that brings you close together.

Obsessive Love

So much for healthy relationships. Now what about the love slave?

The love slave experiences the same addictive chemical response as the woman or man in a healthy relationship. But he or she is bringing an extra dimension to bear. The love slave is what I call a puppet of the past. Experiences and attitudes left over from childhood are pulling the strings of the love slave's adult life.

For example, there was Sharon, a woman who came from a home where her parents were constantly experiencing problems in their daily lives. They came from a small town in New England where both of her parents worked for a clothing mill that went out of business. They lost their home and eventually had to leave the area in search of work. He found a job in a plant manufacturing parts for automobiles, only to be laid off a year after he started working there. Demand for the parts was down, and the new hires were the first to be let go until matters improved. She was also working, though in a restaurant near the plant. Within three weeks of the layoffs that affected her husband, she was also given notice. Business dropped when the plant reduced its staff, and the owner was cutting back to minimum help.

Their lives continued in a similar pattern. They moved from city to city, trying their hand at whatever they could find. Sometimes one of them returned to school, taking courses on computers, electronics, or whatever seemed to provide the greatest opportunities. At other times they did manual labor. They kept food on the table and were never homeless, but their lives seemed hopeless. They knew things would never get better for them, that life would always be only as secure as the next paycheck.

"I was their happiness," Sharon told me. "I was what they called their 'little ray of sunshine in the perpetual storm cloud of their lives.' I was expected to be a good girl, to be helpful, to make dinner, do the dishes, do my homework, and hold a part-time job when I was old enough to work. I was supposed to cheer them up. And I did it all. At least I tried to do it all. God, how I tried.

"It was a ridiculous burden for a growing child, yet somehow I came to feel responsible for everything that happened. I remember one time when we were living near Pittsburgh, I had gone over to play with a friend rather than fixing dinner. My parents came home exhausted and were irate with me. They told me I was ungrateful, that I didn't care about them, about their problems. They said I was selfish. Then, the next day, my mother got laid off where she was working and I somehow blamed myself. I thought that because I had been a bad little girl, her boss had gotten mad at her.

"I tried to help more than before. I tried to work extra hard to make everything right, but my mother told me there was nothing I could do to make things right. She had lost yet another job and nothing would ever be good for them again. It was a statement of hopelessness with no basis in fact, but this was my mother and I believed everything she said.

"I blamed myself. I knew I had failed. My job was to make my parents happy, to keep them from being depressed, to make them laugh, to make them feel better. That's how I viewed my role in the family, and even when I was working my way through college, having almost no money, I tried to send them whatever I could to help. It was ridiculous. I was sharing a hell-hole apartment with three other girls, getting by on two meals a day at best, and trying to be responsible for helping them. I just felt that was my role in life."

It was probably inevitable that Sharon would be drawn to men like her father. They were always depressed, always the kind to snatch defeat from the jaws of victory. There was nothing clinically wrong with them; they were simply men with such low self-esteem that they deliberately sabotaged everything they did.

If they were doing well on a new job, they would take time off when it would most upset the schedules of others. If they were doing well in school, they would cut just enough classes to fall behind, lowering their grades or being forced to take incompletes for the semester. If a relationship was going well, they would begin to "forget" a date, or show up dressed inappropriately so that they would either be embarrassed or have to go home to change, making them uncomfortably late.

Each time there was a problem or a failure, the men would feel terrible. They would berate themselves in front of her, tell her they should break off—"A man like me just isn't good enough for someone like you, Sharon"—or otherwise stress their depression. In reality, the men wanted Sharon to act as a rescuer, to comfort them for what they had set themselves up to receive. Yet she never realized she was being manipulated. She had to ease their depression, to make them feel better—receiving their love only when she was successful. (In therapy she came to see that her parents played a similar game, many of their lay-offs or firings being the result of their deliberate actions. She didn't know whether they consciously or unconsciously tried to fail, but she did see that their lives had been a sham, that they had used her in ways no child should be manipulated.)

At first the relationship would seem to be growing. She would become close to the man, their lives more and more intertwined. The man would seem to come out of his depression as their love for each other blossomed. Yet the good Sharon experienced was nothing more than the normal high of the phenylethylamine. As time passed, the depression would return and the man would grow increasingly manipulative.

"It used to be so good between us, Sharon. Why did you change? Why can't you be like you used to be?" were typical comments. And Sharon, certain from the way she was raised that she must have been at fault, worked even harder. She desperately did whatever the man asked, determined to make him happy in order to hold his love. She never realized that there was no way to make such a person happy in the manner she fantasized.

"I thought I could bring him out of his depression, help him become a success in whatever he wanted to do, and together we would live happily ever after," Sharon told me. "I thought he wanted to be equal partners in life, and it was my job to elevate him to that level. I knew that each time one of my lovers became more demanding, more critical of my failings, that I should leave him. But I just couldn't. I had to succeed. I had to change him. I had to stop failing the men I became serious about. With each new man I told myself that this time things would be different.

"My friends told me I was nuts. They said I was being used. Yet I thought they were the ones who were wrong. I thought I had to assure the success of the relationship. I never thought about the man's responsibility in all this. It just never crossed my mind."

Sharon, seduced by her body's natural amphetamines, masked her love addiction in the early stages of the relationship. She saw genuine change in the men she loved over the years, yet they, too, were only temporarily reacting to body chemistry. When their true personalities were revealed, the men were like puppeteers pulling the strings of a marionette. And Sharon was that puppet of her past, reacting to men as she had learned to react to her father and mother. Only when she understood that she was not responsible for anyone's life but her own did she begin to heal. And only when she realized that her parents had been wrong, that she had been worthy of love all along, that they had been too involved with themselves to truly get to know her, did she change her dating pattern. Today she is engaged to be married to a fine, supportive man who loves her and wants to work with her in life, not use her. He gives as much or more than he receives, and they have a healthy respect for each other.

When Obsession Turns Deadly

The deadly side of obsessive love is not new. Police blotters are filled with the stories of—typically—men who did violence to women because of their obsession. Sometimes the family will blame the victim, saying that "Jim was a one-woman man, and it about broke his heart when she ran off with someone else." Or they might say, "She led him on until I guess he couldn't take it any more."

There are any number of excuses used by those involved, and most blame the victim, although he or she was completely inno-cent. In some instances, when the victim was crippled or disfigured rather than being killed, the assailant then married her. This is seen as "proof" of his remorse and his devotion. He was so "deeply in love" that he just "went crazy." Fortunately the woman finally "came to her senses," understood how serious he was, and, once she forgave him for the (pick one) knife slashes, acid burns, setting her home on fire, beating, shooting, etc., they lived happily ever after. Or so goes the myth surrounding an extremely disturbed family dynamic.

Although acts of violence can point to mental illness, the obviously mentally disturbed individual is not the problem for most women. There are other relationships where the depth of obsessive love, and its dangers, become obvious only at the time when the relationship seems to end.

For example, there was the case of Georgia and Arnold. They worked together on a newspaper as general assignment reporters for two years before they started dating. They had always been friendly in the office, and they had each admired the other's writing. There was no competitiveness between them, their special interests being quite different. She handled science features in addition to her regular duties, and his special expertise was in business. They had each won awards, each earned about the same amount of money, and each had similar futures in the profession.

The relationship started after Georgia entered Arnold's computer file one morning after he came to work wearing a present from his niece and nephew. She found an article he was working on for the Sunday magazine and added, "I like your new tie, Arnie. I've never seen one that glows in the dark before."

He was annoyed that she had broken into his system, since each reporter's file had a personal coded password, but he was pleased she had gone to the trouble of playing a joke on him. He asked her to dinner, took her to a candlelit restaurant, and, when she was struggling to read the menu, removed his tie, saying it might help her see more easily.

That was the start. He told her about his sister and her two children. He told about his parents being dead and how he had made his sister's family his own. He talked about the other places he had worked during his career, and how he had always been lonely after his parents died when he was still in high school. He knew he'd never leave the city because, with his sister's family, he felt like he had some roots.

Georgia's parents lived in Florida, and she neither saw them very often nor spoke to them much by telephone. They were an active, vibrant couple who had always looked upon having children as a necessity for social convention. Her father was a doctor, her mother a professor of law. They were just old enough so the idea of having careers without children was considered selfish. The fact that they hired a nanny and a cook so they would not have to be bothered just made them seem "clever" to their friends. They were able to enjoy a full rich life together and had become socially prominent, frequently going to one charity function or another, always leaving Georgia in the capable hands of sitters who seemed to care for her more than either parent. Once Georgia went off to college, her parents felt their job was over. And when she went into a career neither of them found particularly interesting, they were quite comfortable staying estranged from each other.

Georgia was never certain just when Arnold began taking over her life. Her car broke down one morning and she called him to get a ride in to work. He checked under the hood and told her that what needed fixing was simple. He could do it the next day when he was off from work, something to which she agreed. He arrived early enough to loan her his car, and she brought an elaborate spread of carry-out Chinese food for them to share as a way of thanking him.

Soon Arnold was either spending much of his free time with Georgia, if they had the same days off, or doing chores for her. She had purchased a small, older house that was affordable because it was barely habitable. The wiring and plumbing were new, but everything else needed patching, repairing, replacement, and/or painting. She found working on the house to be relaxing. He was skilled with tools and soon had a key to her place, where he stripped old wallpaper from the walls, refinished her floors, repaired window frames, and generally made himself useful.

At first Georgia was embarrassed by the work he was doing, especially when their days off did not match and she was not around to help him. Eventually he became like a habit, and neither was surprised when she suggested that, if he was going to work on her living room that evening, it might be simpler for him just to sleep over. He had brought a change of clothes, she had an extra toothbrush, and he never really returned to his apartment after that.

The affair was an intense one, Arnold eager to please and Georgia delighted that someone truly cared about her. He would do whatever she wanted. He seemed only to want to make her happy. And then, six weeks after they were living together, he suggested they get married. "We both have some time off. The paper will survive a week without us. And we can probably trade a great honeymoon suite somewhere for a story for the 'Travel' section."

Georgia wasn't certain. She liked him, yet things seemed to be moving too fast. She wanted some time to sit back and think about their relationship, about what she thought of him for the long term. She was embarrassed to say so, embarrassed because, although she had had a couple of serious relationships in the past, she had never lived with a man before. Somehow it seemed as though, if you took that step, marriage should be inevitable. Yet nothing felt quite right.

"Let's wait a little while," she told him. "I think I love you, but this is just too sudden for me."

That was when he told her that he had already requested, and received, the time off. He had contacted the hotel. He knew a minister who would be willing to marry them, and he had set a date. There was no backing out. At least that was what he thought.

"I can't say I was very nice about it," Georgia later commented. "In fact, I just freaked. Our living together was an open secret. We were still at that stage in the relationship where we were obvious to everyone. We'd leave each other cutesy notes, and of course we'd arrive to work at the same time each day since we'd both leave the house at the same time. The fact that we needed separate cars to get around to cover assignments didn't change anything. Everybody knew.

"But that didn't mean that I wanted him to unilaterally decide that he could control the relationship. He had no right to ask for time off for me. He had no right to plan a marriage without proposing marriage. Hell, he had no right to do anything without consulting me first. I don't know what I would have said had he suggested it. I do know I had no intention of marrying him when he was so . . . rude, I guess, is the best way I can put it. I told him there was no way in hell I was going to marry him under such circumstances.

"And that was his turn to freak. He told me he loved me. He told me he was devoted to me. He told me he considered us married the first night he stayed over at my place. He told me he had told his sister all about me, had gotten her encouragement. He told me I *had* to marry him. He couldn't handle rejection. It was too much like how he felt when his parents died."

Arnold refused to move. Georgia began sleeping on the couch in the living room, hoping he would get the hint. When that didn't work, she waited until she had a day off when he had to work, then had a locksmith change the locks on all the doors. She placed all his clothing and other possessions in the garage, along with her key to his apartment. Then she called him at work to tell him what she had done. She also telephoned their employer to explain that she would not be taking any time off to be married, that the relationship had ended.

"He never came for his clothing, his books, any of the stuff he had moved to my place. When I asked him about it, he just said that if he couldn't have me, his life was over anyway. He'd get by. I could just put it in the trash for all he cared. So I did. Maybe he was going to be a martyr, but that didn't mean I had to play his stupid games."

Arnold did not abandon Georgia the way he abandoned his possessions. He told their coworkers at the paper that the marriage had just been delayed because of the deadline pressures of stories they were working on. He left information on an area department store's bridal registry on Georgia's desk. He began deliberately trying to be in the elevator when she was going to or coming from work. And he would go by her house on evenings and weekends, cruising slowly, sometimes parking his car for a few minutes across the street. If he saw an unfamiliar car in the drive, he would go to a pay telephone and call, just to see if she had a man visiting her.

At first Georgia thought of putting her home up for sale. Then she realized that she could not be the victim of an ex-lover who was "acting like a jerk." Each time he parked across the street, she called the police. Eventually, rather than getting involved in what they considered an ongoing domestic quarrel, they advised her to get a restraining order, which she did.

Arnold turned to telephone calls. He told Georgia that no man could ever love her the way he did. He worshiped the ground she walked on. Her mind and body had ruined him for any other woman. "He was half trying to be seductive, half whining like a little boy who discovers that the sun, moon, and stars don't shine only because of him. I began to wonder what I had ever seen in him. I also bought an answering machine so I could screen my calls, something I had never done before because it somehow seemed rude."

Gradually Arnold's actions turned verbally abusive. He said that he had been watching her, that he knew she wasn't dating again. He said it was because everyone knew she was nothing but a "cock-tease," the kind of woman who leads a man on and then dumps him.

"It was a side of Arnie I had never seen. He began criticizing everything about me. He said my arms were too fat, that I had bad breath in the morning, that I looked like a frump at the paper. It was as though he was probing, trying to find where I was emotionally vulnerable, then hone in for the kill.

"Eventually I decided to look for another job, to sell the house I had loved so much, to start over in a new city. My publisher was shocked. She offered to relocate Arnie to one of the other papers in the chain for which we worked. She said he hadn't done enough to warrant firing, but if it ever came to that, she felt he was the one to go, not me.

"Things had gone too far. I didn't know what he would say or do next. I didn't know what the rest of the staff thought about me, about us. And I hated the idea that every time the telephone rang, every time I heard the doorbell, every time I started to look out my front window at the street, I got a catch in my chest. I was over-stressed all the time. No one had the right to have such power over my emotions, and I saw no way to get control other than to just walk away from the nightmare that son of a bitch created."

Georgia was fortunate. When she moved to a new job in a different city, Arnold made only a half-hearted effort to learn where she went, then got involved with another woman at the paper.

Other stalkers remain obsessed, unable to let go. Some become vicious, doing things like mailing copies of nude pictures of the loved one to any new lover. Others slash tires, commit arson, or otherwise make indirect physical assaults. Other times, the violence is more than a threat. Men are not the only ones who can turn into aggressors. In fact, the average male victim of a stalker can be even more helpless than a woman. He may be embarrassed to go to the police, whose typical reaction is, "I should have such problems, buddy," or "You sure you're not just bragging?" If she becomes violent, the question becomes one of knowing when physical self-defense is acceptable and when he will be considered to have committed assault and battery against her.

The woman may also use sexual blackmail, threatening to accuse the man of rape. If the couple has had a child, she may threaten to claim child abuse or child molestation. It is such a seemingly twisted way to force the man to return to an intimate relationship that it is often overlooked by the prosecutors until the truth comes out in trial. By then it may be too late. The man has already spent a small fortune on legal bills, has had his name in the paper, and is likely to be presumed guilty because of society's abhorrence of such crimes.

This is not to say that such approaches are common. Fortunately they are not. The vast majority of date rape, spousal rape, and lover rape accusations are quite valid. Likewise, children are rarely thrown into the middle of an obsessive love pursuit. But a woman is more likely to make such changes than a man, and the man being changed is less likely to obtain sympathy from the courts.

No matter what the form of stalking, this is not the moonstruck, starry-eyed lover who cannot keep himself from driving or walking down the street that is home to his beloved. This is not the woman who writes love notes and takes up the pursuit of sports she previously hated to please her man. This is the act of someone who has gone beyond the lines of propriety.

Stalkers are usually emotionally disturbed, and there is a great risk of physical danger from them, regardless of who they are. Many states have developed stalker laws to allow for the prosecution of such crimes. Many cities have police officers trained to handle this form of potential violence. If you are being stalked, this book may provide some insight, but you cannot fight a stalker alone. Such obsessive lovers need to be stopped through legal means. See your police, city, and/or county prosecutor at once. When obsession turns to stalking, lives are at risk.

Chapter 3

Recognizing Love Addiction

In the last chapter we examined what can happen when love addiction goes too far. Fortunately, the darkest side of obsessive love is rare. You are more likely to experience problems similar to those of Sharon, the rescuer, who began to change when she discovered she was a love addict. And that discovery came from her taking a test I devised and have administered to thousands of people dealing with relationship problems over the years. It is a foolproof way to learn whether you are a puppet of your past. Before you read any further, I suggest you take a piece of paper and a pencil and see where you stand in your relationships.

Are You a Love Slave?
The questions that follow cover the twenty-five traits of obsessive love. Number your paper from one to twenty-five, then take the test, writing "yes" or "no" for each question. Everyone is likely to have one or more of these traits, so an occasional positive answer is not cause for concern. At the end of the test, I will explain how to interpret your score.

The Questions
(Please Note: The reference to a "love object" in the questions refers to a boyfriend or girlfriend, a live-in lover, or a spouse, as appropriate for your specific circumstances.)

1. Do you have low self-esteem when you are alone and not involved with a loved one? Do you feel as though you are no good? Are you in a position where you have a high income and are regularly praised for the quality of your work, yet you feel that neither the income nor the respect are deserved? That you are a fraud waiting to be unmasked? That you frequently feel a sense of desolation? If you are in a routine or lower-paying job, do you believe that is all you deserve, all you are worth?

2. Do you look to others to make you happy? Do you feel that there can be no happiness just being alone with yourself?

3. Do you feel that you need a woman or a man to make your life seem fulfilled?

4. Are you obsessed with finding the right mate? Is this your primary goal in life?

5. Are you needy? Do you constantly need assurance, love, and a sense of security from others, especially your love object?

6. Are you constantly worried about satisfying your mate?

7. Are you possessive, jealous, envious of others?

8. Do you have a fear of loneliness?

9. Do you project all of your hopes and dreams onto your love object?

10. Do you place your love object on a pedestal? Do you believe that anything that person says about you and your relationship together must be correct? Do you feel that he or she is special to the point of being almost beyond reproach?

11. Do you have a sexual problem? This may be frigidity if you are a woman and either impotence or the fear of impotence if you are a man. (This question refers strictly to a physical problem of psychological origin, not a problem that requires medical or surgical correction.)

12. No matter how intense your feelings for your love object, do you eventually find yourself losing the person? Or, if you are involved with your first serious relationship, have you noticed a marked or dramatic change in the other person? Is there tension where previously there had been no problems? Do you feel that the other person is no longer happy with you? (Anyone who has had more than one such love object will recognize these as possible signs of impending loss.)

13. Do you give up your individuality for your love object? Do you try to become the person he or she desires instead of expressing your true feelings and interests?

14. Do you constantly fear that your partner may leave you? Do even the most minor arguments fill you with dread that

your partner may not desire to stay in the relationship any longer? Do you become worried when your love object is delayed, fearing that the person has decided never to return?

15. Do you still hunger for a closeness to one or both parents that you lacked during early childhood? Did you perceive yourself to be unloved and/or unwanted and/or uncared for when growing up? If you were a victim of incest, you should score this question with a "yes."

16. Do you feel dependent? If you are a female, do you feel that if you assert your independence, you will lose your love object?

17. Have you picked the wrong mate? This may seem an easy question at first glance, if your tendency is to feel that the love object is perfect while you are worthless. But does your love object deliberately make you feel miserable most of the time?

18. Are you extremely romantic? Do you feel that romance conquers all, perhaps assuring happiness if pursued correctly?

19. Are you an escapist? Do you find fantasy more pleasurable than your reality, and thus something to cling to?

20. Do you have difficulty handling stress?

21. Do you seem to have a low immune system? Do you get colds a lot? Do you get flu a lot? If some "bug" is "going around," are you someone who is fairly certain to get sick, even though others around you always seem to stay healthy?

22. Do you have a poor self-image? No matter what your appearance, do you feel that you never look quite right? If someone compliments you, do you feel that they are lying to you, mocking you, or don't really know what they are talking about? Also score "yes" for this question if you feel that the only way you can attract the opposite sex is through an attraction other than your personality and current appearance, such as money, a fancy car, an expensive home or apartment, or some other "thing."

23. Are you a "sex slave?" Do you feel safe, warm, and desired primarily when you are having sex? Will you do whatever is necessary to ensure that your love object will want to have

sex with you? In some instances a love addict will be intensely demanding. In other instances he or she will be subservient, willing to do anything to be allowed to go to bed with the love object. The important point is that in sex there is a feeling of love and acceptance that seems lacking at most other times.

24. Do you depend upon others for love instead of loving yourself? Loving yourself does not mean you are a narcissist. A narcissist is someone who feels that he or she is the center of the universe. It is an extreme situation that has nothing to do with normal, healthy self-love. Self-love means self-approval, self-acceptance, the knowledge that your life was not some sort of cosmic mistake or universal joke. You have value just as others do. You can love others, interact, and accept love in return. Such characteristics are impossible for the love addict.

25. Do you use alcohol, marijuana, cocaine, or other drugs to avoid looking at your current or past relationships? Do you use drugs to avoid seeing your love object for the way he or she might be in real life? And/or have you had one or more affairs in order to avoid feeling a full commitment to your love object and/or to avoid talking with your love object about problems between you? Likewise, if your love object has had an affair, are you afraid to confront this problem for fear that he or she will no longer want you, no longer want to work on the relationship?

SCORING: If you answered "yes" to six or fewer of these characteristics, then you are a person who may or may not have experienced occasional relationship difficulties in your past, though no more often than anyone who is healthy and normal. You are definitely NOT a love addict and can enjoy a healthy, caring, and committed relationship without counseling, working this program, or any outside assistance.

If you answered "yes" to at least seven of these questions, then you are a borderline love addict who is functioning within the normal range. Working the exercises that follow may make your relationships easier to handle, but the exercises are not crucial for your future. A score of nine "yes" answers indicates that you may be functioning with little difficulty, but would be wise to work the program. You are a candidate for relationship problems at some period during your life if you do not take action now.

Twelve "yes" answers means you are a love addict. This problem has already interfered with your current and past relationships, though you may not be aware of this fact.

Any score over fifteen means that your life is controlled by your love addiction. This program is crucial for your present and any future relationship.

Common Traits of Love Addicts
No matter how you may have scored on the test, there are some common traits of all love addicts. The kind of life you lead when you are trapped by obsessive love—either your own or that of someone close to you—will vary. But the traits you or any love slave exhibit will be consistent regardless of your income, education, job, age, sex, sexual orientation, or racial or ethnic background.

The love addict is someone who feels responsible for other people's feelings, thoughts, actions, choices, and sense of well-being or the lack thereof. He or she feels anxiety, pity, or guilt when other people have a problem, then feels compelled, almost forced, to help that person solve the problem, becoming angry if that help proves ineffective.

The love addict anticipates other people's needs and wonders why others don't do the same for him or her. Addicts find themselves saying "yes" when they mean "no," then feel compelled to be involved with activities and/or relationships with which they are not fully comfortable. But rather than complain, they may allow themselves to be further used, often engaging in projects where they find themselves doing more than their fair share of the work.

The love addict constantly craves the other person's attention. He is extremely uncomfortable when alone. In the extreme, the addict cannot be alone—he must have the other person around. Panic and hysteria may be experienced during periods of separation from the love object, so every effort is made to avoid that separation. Sometimes this means surprising a lover or spouse by going to the city where she has traveled for business. At other times, when there is no way to be together for a few days, the love addict will deliberately overindulge in activities, working until complete exhaustion allows him to sleep.

Love addicts either do not know what they want or need or, if they know, tell themselves that their wants and needs are not important. They frequently diminish their own worth and exaggerate the value of the loved one. Thus they may become angry over injustices done to others, taking whatever actions are necessary to right such wrongs, but ignore injustices done to themselves. They feel safest when giving; insecure and guilty when something is done for them. At the same time, when they reflect on their lives, they are saddened by the fact that nothing was given to them, while they spent their lives giving to others.

Such individuals find themselves attracted only to needy people because they find that needy people are attracted to them. They feel their lives are boring and empty if they don't have a crisis to handle, a problem to solve, someone to help. They rally to causes that will help others, overcommitting, then feeling harried and pressured.

Yet there is no sense of personal responsibility for their unhappiness. They blame others for the spot they feel they are in and the emotions they are experiencing. They may feel that other people are driving them crazy. They may feel angry, victimized, unappreciated. They have low self-worth, usually coming from troubled, repressed, or dysfunctional families, though they will deny this fact. Instead, they blame themselves for everything including the way they think, look, and behave.

Should others criticize the love addict, he will become angry, self-righteous, and indignant. He rejects compliments and praise, then becomes depressed when he no longer receives such praise and compliments. He feels as though he is an outsider in the world, as though it is wrong for him to spend money on himself, even on necessities.

Love addicts have usually been victims of emotional, physical, or sexual abuse, or abandonment. There may also be alcoholism and/or drug dependency within the family. Frequently the love addict's first serious relationship will be with someone who is physically and/or emotionally abusive, and/or a substance abuser. Sometimes there is the feeling that the person "needs" the love addict or that no one else understands him. Other times the relationship results from the love addict's subconscious belief that he does not deserve anyone any better.

Love addicts often feel like victims. They believe that they can do nothing right. They are afraid of making mistakes, expect to do everything perfectly, then wonder why they have a tough time making decisions. They never seem to be able to get things done to their own satisfaction. They live with guilt, with the sense that they should always be doing something more, doing something different. They are ashamed of who they are, feel that their lives aren't worth living, and prefer trying to help other people live their lives instead. Their sense of self-worth comes only from helping others, holding in disdain anything they may do for themselves.

Love addicts do not believe anyone could like or love them, yet desperately want others to have such emotions towards them. They believe that good things will not happen to them and that they do not deserve good things happening to them.

Love addicts are repressed, often rigid and controlled. They are anxious about the difficulties of others, frequently talking about such problems, no matter how minor. They lose sleep over the behavior and concerns of others, bearing a burden that should not be theirs. They worry that the other person isn't going to love them. They worry that their actions will push the other person away, that they can't satisfy the other person, that they will be left, rejected, the other person finding someone else. There is a constant fear of loneliness, of losing love.

Love addicts focus all their energy on other people, then wonder why they never have any energy for themselves, why they never seem to be able to get things done. They often become controlling, afraid to allow events to happen naturally. They think they know best how events should turn out and how people should behave. They try to control events and people through helplessness, guilt, coercion, advice giving, manipulation, and domination. They become frustrated and angry. They feel controlled by events and people. They ignore problems or pretend they are not happening. They tell themselves that things will be better tomorrow. They stay busy so they will not have to think about it.

Often the love addict becomes confused, depressed, and/or sick. She may take tranquilizers or alcohol, spend too much money, or overeat—then pretend such behaviors are not happening. She believes lies and lies to herself, then wonders why she fears she is going crazy. And she always feels that happiness is going to come from outside, from getting love from somebody, anybody. She doesn't care who the person might be so long as he says it is love. She doesn't care what the other person does to her so long as there is a sense of being loved. She will suffer anything—from physical or emotional abuse to flaunting extra-marital affairs—just so long as the other person loves her. And even as she desperately seeks love and approval, she frequently chooses people who are incapable of giving that love.

Love addicts usually come to equate love with pain. Since the person they select is the wrong one, they have endless opportunities to try and make themselves "better" or "more worthy." Since they secretly don't think they are worthy of love, they don't take the time to see whether other people are good for them. And because they are so worried about how other people see them, they don't take the time to decide whether or not they love or like other people. They look to relationships to supply their happiness and so they will stay in relationships that don't work, even to the point of tolerating extreme abuse to keep people "loving" them. And always they wonder whether they will ever find "real love."

Communication is extremely difficult for love addicts. They are constantly trying to say the right thing, to say the words that will get people to love them. They have trouble forming their thoughts because they dare not offend.

Conversations are seldom personal. Love addicts talk about others, not themselves, unless they feel the need to speak against themselves. They feel that their opinions don't really matter. They feel as though they are intruding on others, so they will let other people hurt them. All that matters is that the people doing the hurting say that they love them.

Love addicts don't trust themselves, their decisions, or others. If they have been raised in a religious background, they will privately admit that they have come to distrust God. They say that God has abandoned them. As a result, they feel scared, hurt, and angry, yet frightened of that anger because they believe it might drive others from them.

Sex, for love addicts, is seldom pleasurable, although they will have sex whenever and however the partner desires. They often try to have sex when they are angry or hurt. They frequently refuse to enjoy sex because they feel that their partners do not love them enough. They are afraid of losing control, and have a difficult time asking for the fulfillment they are seeking in bed. They may withdraw emotionally from the partner, feeling revulsion for that person yet believing that they have to provide all the sex desired so the partner will give them love. In some instances sex is reduced to a mechanical act, devoid of all feelings, despite what they might otherwise desire.

The love addict will frequently have an extramarital affair. Such affairs restore their sense of being loved. They also frequently lead to the destruction of their primary relationships, making them feel as though they are martyrs. The fact that they caused the problem by having the affair is often overlooked.

When love addicts do seek help, it is usually for symptoms such as the depression that comes from repressing their anger, overeating, inappropriate, periodic bouts of rage, or some similar difficulty. There are also instances when love addicts become sex addicts, and that behavior leads either to therapy or to the joining of a twelve-step program such as Sexaholics Anonymous.

The Problem of Avoidance

One reason love addicts often fail to recognize their circumstances is that it is so easy for an adult to justify an unpleasant situation. For example, if every intimate relationship is ultimately an unfulfilling disaster, the love addict often blames the partner. "How can I find happiness when no man wants to have a meaningful relationship?" is typical of the questions I receive from love addicts. Or "I bend over backward to please them, then they say I don't understand them. Well, they're right. Today's women just don't want a loving, caring man who supports them in what they do."

There is also a tendency on the part of the adult love addict to discount or "forget" the childhood pain that gave rise to all his difficulties. He views the past without the perspective of the child whose reaction to those early life experiences shaped the adult relationship. It stands to reason that the fewer the experiences one has had, the greater the impact of those experiences. When an adult gets a new job in a different city, for example, the excitement of the relocation, the challenge of the work, and the higher pay make the move a positive event. The adult has also learned from other moves that each new apartment or home brings its own special pleasures, from making new friends to establishing a fresh living environment. But for a small child, a move means the loss of everything familiar. There are frequently no past experiences from which to draw comfort, and the child is terrified, angry, and hurt by suddenly being thrown out of control.

The adult love addict often suppresses the memory of the pain of those early childhood experiences. In hindsight, things often "weren't so bad." There is an adult understanding, not only of what was experienced, but also how much pain others had in their childhoods. In this way the root cause of the love addiction is often overlooked, and the victim spends his or her time searching for reasons in ways that do not matter.

Phyllis had such a childhood. Her father was a mid-level corporate executive in a manufacturing company whose product line was increasingly not competitive. He made excellent money, allowing his wife to have the choice of staying home with their daughter. The family owned a large house, and a maid came by to clean three days a week.

If there were problems, they were ones of inadvertent neglect. Phyllis' father, believing that a man's work was a measure of his worth, routinely arrived home after his wife and daughter had eaten dinner. Her mother, meanwhile, was on tranquillizers for allergies, often leaving her lethargic and unable to be active with her daughter.

Phyllis felt happy, knowing she was loved, but was also lonely at times. Most of the children in her immediate neighborhood were either older or younger than herself, so that there was seldom anyone her own age to play with. Television and books became Phyllis' friends. She delighted in the romantic parts of the stories that she watched, and the stories were ones quite typical of the 1950s. The plots regularly revealed that a woman was to find happiness in marriage. Mr. Right made everything perfect. The films and television shows were like fairy tales where "happily ever after" always meant being cared for by the man. There was no greater aspiration for a woman than to be "fulfilled" by a man's love.

The novels she read were the same—never looking past the moment of wedding bliss, of the commitment of man to woman "till death do they part." There were never any arguments, never a divorce, never a need to explain the relationship. Marriage was a time of enchantment, and "I do" were the magic words that swept you into the perfect kingdom. Sometimes the novels were contemporary stories. Sometimes they were fantasy or historical in nature. Whatever the case, the message was always one of happiness only possible with a man. A woman might desire or even seek a career, as Phyllis herself did after college, but everything was somewhat empty without that perfect relationship.

Whether or not Phyllis' actions might have had long-term consequences with no other changes occurring cannot be known. There was nothing obsessive about her early enjoyment of television shows, movies, and books. She was passing the time as best she could in what was a loving but rather lonely childhood.

The change came when Phyllis was eleven and just entering the throes of adolescence. It was a time when there would be a certain amount of emotional turmoil at best. In her case, there was total upheaval. Her father's company analyzed the market they were in, the competition, and the cost of maintaining a successful operation, and decided to go out of business. At the same time, Phyllis' mother became so disabled from her allergies and from reactions to her medication that she could not work. The family income dropped to almost nothing, and her father was frantic to keep everyone together.

The home in which Phyllis was raised was placed on the market immediately, Unfortunately, the economy that had made the sale necessary had also devastated the real estate market. The house was finally sold, but the bank got most of the sale.

The family moved into a two-bedroom apartment in a new community with a different school system. Phyllis was shy about making new friends and embarrassed by her father's misfortune, and withdrew even further into her world of television and novels. At first Phyllis' parents tried to be supportive, being sensitive to what they recognized were additional emotional needs in the time of crisis. But her father, unable to find a job that paid the salary he had been earning, eventually took two jobs, working long hours to provide his daughter with a good education. Phyllis' mother was frequently bedridden, and even during the good periods, when her health permitted her to get around, she stopped meeting her daughter's needs. She seemed to feel that there were only so many hours when she felt well enough to do something for herself. Her daughter was growing rapidly and would soon be going off to college. Phyllis could get along OK without her.

The reality was that Phyllis felt not only unloved but unlovable. She saw herself as having become a child no one cared about. Her father was never home, and while she intellectually understood what was happening, she wanted to tell him that he should spend less time working and more time with her. She valued his time more than his money. She would find a way to get an education. What mattered was his presence in her life. But she never said that, never mentioned the pain. And because she never tried to discuss what was happening, her fantasy life became her primary means of escaping to a more comfortable world. She decided that her only hope for a better future was through meeting her "Prince Charming."

Greg was Phyllis' first serious love. He found her intelligent, witty, and what he called "adaptive." They went to the same university together, and though he held a part-time job, he did not need to work. His father was a successful advertising executive, and Greg's marketing major was the first step toward his eventually taking over the firm.

Greg was self-centered in ways Phyllis wanted to overlook. He was extremely attentive and loving when they were together. He delighted in meeting her in coffee shops, sometimes alone, sometimes with friends, to discuss what they felt were the great issues of the day. They went to concerts and museums, and they took long walks. Yet Greg was easily distracted when he wasn't around Phyllis. There were no other girls in his life, but if he promised Phyllis he would meet her in the library to study and a friend suggested they go for a beer, Greg would not call Phyllis to say he would be late. The same situation occurred at other times, with other activities. He wasn't deliberately self-centered—it was just that once something became "routine" to him, he didn't mind finding some excitement elsewhere. And if he was having a good time or intensely involved with what he was doing, he tended to forget all else. At least that's how he tried to explain his periodic rudeness to her.

Phyllis said that she understood. She justified what he was doing based on her father's actions after he lost his job. A man had to work hard, and if he got absorbed in what he was doing, that just showed his mature dedication to work.

Her friends argued otherwise. It was one thing to excuse his coming late from his job, they told her. And it was certainly possible to get absorbed in research in the library. But Greg was just as likely to be late because he was having a beer with one of his male buddies. She couldn't justify that kind of behavior, could she? But Phyllis said they just didn't understand. Jim Anderson sometimes was delayed on *Father Knows Best*. Ward Cleaver might be late on *Leave It To Beaver*. John Walton, Sr., was forever delayed returning to the family home on Walton's Mountain.

Television is not real life, Phyllis' friends told her. She said she knew better.

There were factors at play with Greg as well. His father, a self-made success story with little time for his family, had had a number of affairs over the years, sometimes with his son's awareness, sometimes not. But Greg adored his father, and in trying to imitate the older man's success, adopted his attitudes toward women. His idea of a relationship did not involve mutual respect.

The more Phyllis accepted Greg's lax attitude toward their dates, the closer they became. She felt insecure, determined to hang on until marriage, when everything would be perfect. The wedding ceremony would release the true character of her beloved, like a genie being released from a bottle. It was as though she was being tested by some higher power she accepted without fully understanding.

Greg likewise grew closer to Phyllis. She acted as a woman was supposed to act. After all, his mother had made a comfortable life for herself, living off her husband. She had money. She had friends. She was lucky her husband didn't divorce her, as was happening with so many other parents of his friends. Phyllis understood her place in a relationship, and their life would be better than his father had it because Phyllis would earn her own way, not be a "leech" like his mother.

Phyllis and Greg were puppets of their past. Greg was selfish and immature. Phyllis was a love addict. She was desperate for male approval and male attention because of the loneliness of her teen-aged years. She was trying to recapture what she had missed, making a mistake she would come to repeat before she happened into a seminar I was giving.

I met Phyllis after her third experience with men like Greg. Although she never married Greg, they had moved in together and set a date for their wedding when she discovered he was having a "meaningless affair" (his words, she told me) with his father's receptionist. Dave was her second love, a resident in neurosurgery at an area hospital, with a wife he conveniently forgot to mention. And her third relationship, the one she was in when she came to the seminar, was showing all the signs of being as unsuitable as the first two.

It was during the seminar that Phyllis took the quiz you have just finished taking. That was when she realized she was a love slave, acting like a puppet of her past. Where she had thought of herself as being in control of her own life, she understood that she was reacting to experiences she thought were behind her.

Eventually Phyllis began working the program you will encounter later in this book. When she did, she found that her relationships with men changed. She found herself drawn only to those individuals who treated her with respect for who and what she was. They wanted to share a life with her, not dominate her or be dominated by her. She understood that she could never be happy trying to alter herself or tolerating the intolerable. She did not look for a man to change in order to be "happy ever after." She realized that if a man was wrong for her when they first dated, he would probably be wrong for her in the years to come.

Ending Love Addiction/Ending Relationships?

Can a love addict sustain an existing relationship? This question is often asked by men and women who are married, especially those with children. While the specifics of this will be covered later in this book, as you learn how to recover from love addiction, the answer is that a relationship need not end. It need only be different.

A couple may be right for each other, yet drawn together for the wrong reasons. This is no different than the crisis every healthy relationship faces. You know the pattern: a couple meets, falls in love, and eventually marries. Over time, the so-called "honeymoon period" comes to an end as the husband and wife get to know each other as they really are. For many couples, this is a turning point in the relationship. Traits that had once seemed endearing become annoying. The person who had seemed "quiet" now becomes merely "boring"; the "outgoing" one is suddenly "loud" and "shallow." What went wrong?

Finally there is the point of separation or reconciliation and new romance. The wife may decide, "I will never again live with a man who snores." Or she may decide, "He's faithful, kind, gentle, and adores me. I don't like the snoring, but it is a nightly reminder of how lucky I am to be living with him." The husband may say, "I cannot continue wasting half my life while she sits in the bedroom putting on make-up. I need someone more spontaneous." Or he may say, "I hate the time she takes getting made-up because I think she's beautiful without all that paint. But I know she's trying to look her best for me, and no woman has ever loved me so much as to go to all that trouble."

In other words, after the honeymoon stage, when the blinders are off and we see our partner for the way he or she truly happens to be, we make a fresh decision. We might end the relationship, or in our more objective awareness, we might feel even more positively toward the other person. But whatever we do, the relationship is never the same again.

A similar situation exists for the couple where one or both is love-addicted to the other. Once you stop being a puppet to the past, you look at your partner with new clarity. Sometimes this means that the attraction is gone: the love built on fantasy cannot withstand the light of reality. At other times, the person discovers that the spouse or lover is far better in reality than in fantasy. You fall in love anew, though this time with a real person, not a projected image from childhood or adolescence. The relationship is stronger than ever, and the love can be sustained for many years to come.

No one can predict the outcome. All I can tell you is that, no matter what the ultimate relationship evolving from working this program, when you are no longer a love slave, your life will be happier than ever before.

Chapter 4

The Life of a Love Slave

We have seen that for a love slave, relationships can be difficult or impossible to sustain over the long term. Sooner or later, the addict's behavior becomes so extreme that the healthy partner gets the message, and flees. But what about when two obsessive lovers fall in love with one another? Does it work? Their relationship seems one made in heaven, each worshiping the ground the other walks on. Eventually, however, the same thing happens. They reach the same crisis as every other couple—the difference being that the less extreme partner often fails to realize that he or she has a serious problem.

When Two Love Addicts Fall in Love

Evie and Jack couldn't have been better suited for each other, their friends all agreed. They both worked for a large department store, she in personnel training and he as manager of the furniture department. They enjoyed going to plays and movies and eating out in cheap coffee houses that served what they called "upscale junk food." Their tastes in movies were the same. And they both had similar childhoods.

Evie was one of three children born to a woman who was never able to sustain a relationship. Each child had a different father, whom she married and divorced. Each baby had been proof of God's blessing upon the relationship, her mother believed, and she was always shocked when the marriage did not work out.

The truth was that Evie's mother lived in a fantasy world. She expected her children to fulfill her emotional needs. Each time she gave birth, it was as though she thought she was going to have a perfect child who would sleep through the night, fix his or her own bottle, and change his or her own diaper. She wanted the children to love and nurture her, not the other way around. She had been emotionally neglected in her own childhood, not an uncommon situation for those who are physically or emotionally abusive to their own offspring, and she thought a baby would provide the love she felt herself lacking.

Most likely Evie's mother never loved the men she married. All she really wanted them to do was help her make a baby. She did not believe in premarital sex, but she was never concerned with the quality of the relationship. The shortest marriage was a year, her mother filing for divorce the day after she left the hospital after giving birth to one of Evie's brothers. The longest marriage was three years, and that was to Evie's father. However, she had no memory of what he was like.

None of the men was very regular with his support payments, and Evie grew up at a time when collecting was difficult. Her mother always worked two jobs to make ends meet, certain that life would get better each time there was a change. She filed for bankruptcy to clear herself of debt, then celebrated by burdening herself with too many expenses. She moved into an apartment large enough for each child to have his or her own room, then spent what should have been rent money for partying. She got behind, was evicted, then looked upon moving into newer, smaller, older quarters as a delightful challenge. Again she fell behind, moving to yet another building.

The children quickly learned that they could never trust her word. She was self-centered and acted in whatever she felt might be her own best interests of the moment. They tried not to get too attached to their apartments, to the schools they attended, to other children who might become memories before they became friends. Evie's brother found a kitten, brought it home, and was given permission to keep it. He adored the animal, then was forced to leave it with a neighbor when it was time to start fresh. He never trusted their mother again.

Evie, the youngest, tried desperately to seek control. As a small child she played wishing games. She would say little chants that were meant to assure the outcome she sought in life. She was like a teenager plucking petals from a flower to determine whether "he loves me; he loves me not. He loves me; he loves me not . . ." She hoped somehow to get her mother to come home right after work, to spend time with her, to settle on one father or maybe no more fathers for them at all. But her mother refused to face herself or learn to handle her affairs. Instead, she moved them from one apartment to another, one school to another, sometimes even one city or another.

By the time she was in high school, Evie desperately wanted consistency in her life. Her junior year she fell in love with the tall, gangly boy who was the captain of the school's worst basketball team in ten years. All through the basketball season she attended every practice, every home and away game. He was depressed by his failures. She was willing to console him. She loved him and believed in him, and he loved the way she stayed by him. She knew they would be together "forever," yet that summer her mother moved them to a different school district, and though they telephoned each other, by October the former love of her life was dating someone else.

Evie went away to college in a small New England town where she found the first stability of her life, and she was determined to not be hurt again. She found herself a tiny efficiency apartment she could afford, adopted a cat from the animal shelter, and worked at the check-out counter of the supermarket when she wasn't attending classes. She knew she would never return to her mother, knew she would never allow herself to have a disappointing relationship. She would do whatever was necessary to make a man happy, to earn his love and keep it.

Jack's home life had been just as unstable. His father was a career military man on the rise. He sought every possible assignment, every educational opportunity, as he rose in rank and responsibility. He always told his son that he was married to the country first, and to his mother second. "I love you, boy, but you're growing up fast and one day you'll leave here to go on your own. This country of ours has been around two hundred years, and it's the army that will assure it's still here two hundred years from now. I'm going to do what I can to make it great, and when I retire, your mother will be by my side, while you'll have a life of your own." Essentially Jack's father was telling him that he would ignore him growing up, and he was true to his word.

Jack's childhood was lonely and ever-changing. He frequently went to schools on or just off various military bases throughout the world, where he was exposed to other children just like himself. He did not take advantage of this, however, imagining that somehow they had life better than he did. He became withdrawn, a loner, certain he was unique.

Eventually Jack became involved in the arts, playing the clarinet, acting in school plays, and even trying his hand at stand-up comedy in a local club near his college. He was terrible at everything; even he recognized that his greatest skill would always be as part of the audience. Finally he took the job in the department store. The pay was adequate, and the benefits were excellent.

Selling was difficult for him, yet he proved to be more skilled than his more gregarious coworkers because he genuinely cared what the customers thought about what they bought. He helped them get the best equipment available within their price range; he made certain they were happy. And he developed a loyal, ever-growing following.

Dating Evie was a little like selling appliances for Jack. He was determined to please her, determined to make their relationship increase in intensity. The idea that she might not like some aspect of him was devastating. If she commented that she liked a new tie, he would try to buy only those ties he found that were similar. She said she liked roses, so he arranged for a fresh rose to be in a bud vase on her desk each morning when she arrived at work.

Soon Evie and Jack were intimate, and each agreed that the feelings they were experiencing were more intense than any they had ever thought possible. If there was any tension, it was because they were trying too hard to each please the other. Evie was intensely aroused by a man totally devoted to her every pleasure. Jack kept asking Evie what she enjoyed, then followed her every whim, getting his pleasure from her reaction. Neither was certain the other was honest about their desires and fantasies, but they were thrilled by the fact that the other was so intensely selfless.

"With Evie, I'll never be lonely again," Jack told anyone who would listen.

"How could any woman not want a man who is totally devoted to her every wish?" Evie said to her friends.

The wedding was a modest one. Jack's father did not attend, though he sent a telegram of congratulations. His mother came for a few days before the ceremony, then flew out to join her husband in Europe. She said that she had met her new daughter-in-law and that was all that mattered.

Evie's mother got drunk before the wedding and spent most of the ceremony crying. Evie had located her father and sent him an invitation, but he called to tell her that his new wife did not think his going was appropriate. Then he laughed and said, "Besides, I'm not sure I'd recognize you, though I guess you'll be the only girl there in a long white dress." He did not consider the sad truth of his wisecrack, or how deeply the fact hurt her.

The emotional frustration of the family reaction was offset by the intensity of Jack and Evie's feelings toward each other. Although they had been staying at one apartment or the other for several weeks prior to the wedding, that night they both felt as though they were virgins, having sex for the first time.

Everything was perfect between them at first. Jack was a more effective salesman than ever, because his happiness seemed infectious. Evie found that no matter what the frustrations of the job, she was oblivious. With Jack's love, nothing else mattered. All problems were trivial ones.

Neither was certain when tension first arose between them. Evie remembered watching Jack make a sale to an attractive young woman who told him she had just left home and moved into her first apartment. She thought he was a little too friendly, a little too solicitous, a little too interested in where she lived and where she worked.

He snapped back that he had ignored the way she looked at her supervisor during some of the employee training sessions. He felt that she was flirting with the man, and though he knew it was innocent, he wondered why it was necessary for her to behave that way at all.

Evie said that she had no interest in her supervisor. She had no interest in any man other than Jack. And if she seemed more open and friendly than usual, it was because he had made her so happy.

The argument was over as quickly as it began. Each was ashamed of jumping to conclusions. They went to an expensive restaurant that night, holding hands and intimately stroking one another under the table, hoping the cloth would hide what they were doing from the awareness of the other diners. They were successful, but they became so excited that they spent much of the night making love.

All seemed to be going well once again until Evie received a promotion. She was to be trained in worker relations and assigned to handle union negotiations for a contract that was soon to be renewed. Jack told her that she was good at her job, but that nobody he knew thought she was *that* good. He said that she must have done something special to deserve it.

Annoyed, she told him that she was the mistress of the Chairman of the Board of the department store chain—a man in his late eighties, in frail health, and soon to be replaced by the current president of the company.

Instead of realizing that Evie was being facetious, Jack said, "Not all men want sex. Some old guys just like the idea of a pretty young woman on their arm."

"I was joking!" she yelled, shocked, angry, and dismayed. What kind of a fool was he? "I'm not having an affair with anyone. I don't even think he knows I exist, Jack. For God's sake, do you think I'm some kind of slut or something?"

"I think you're very ambitious," he said. "Like my father. He'd do anything to make the Joint Chiefs of Staff. You're a lot like him."

Evie later told me that she felt as though she had been slapped in the face. Not only was she horrified by his statements, she worried that she might really be that ambitious. She analyzed her life and her career and she looked at the way she had been treated when growing up. Finally she realized that there was no basis for what he had said, that he had been needlessly hurtful.

"I asked him if he wanted a divorce," Evie said. "I asked him if he wasn't happy with me any more. I asked him if there was someone else in his life."

Jack was suddenly as horrified as Evie. He wondered how she could think that of him. Sure, he had been jealous. He had been worried. She was beautiful. She was intelligent. She was everything a man could want in a woman, while he was nothing but a sales clerk with a future that would never be much different from his present.

"I told him that he loved me, and that meant more to me than if he was Prince Charles of England."

"Diana hated Prince Charles. She cheated on him," Jack reminded her, suddenly crying uncontrollably.

"He told me he loved me. He told me he couldn't stand the idea of living without me. He said his life would be empty, like one of the cardboard television sets used in the department store's sample bedroom furniture displays. I was so much a part of him, he could never have a complete life without me. Surely I understood all that. Then we both cried, both held each other. And that night we might have been on our honeymoon together again."

Evie had thought everything was over. She trusted Jack and Jack trusted her. She found reason to come down to the furniture department to see him during the day, and he found reason to stop by personnel from time to time. But she said they were only celebrating their love, not spying on one another.

The pressures intensified between them. They were jealous, and as is the case with all relationships where both parties are love-addicted, one of the parties soon became more suspicious than the other. In this case it was Jack, though it is just as likely to be the woman who gets carried away.

Jack felt he could no longer trust Evie. He thought that the training programs she had been giving for several years might actually be a cover for an illicit affair. He paid one of the department store's security guards to follow her when he was off duty and she had to do work in a branch store. Evie did nothing to warrant such suspicion, and the security guard laughed to his friends that it was the easiest $100 he ever made. Soon word got back to Evie, and she was irate. At the same time, Jack worried that maybe it was the security guard with whom Evie was having the affair. Maybe the money he paid the guard financed an illicit rendezvous.

The opposite of love is not hate. It is indifference, a far more tragic state of affairs. It was not long before Evie was as void of passion as she had once thrilled to the most casual touch of her beloved. They still had sex, though suddenly it was mechanical on her part. They went out to eat. They talked about their jobs, about people they knew at work. They were very polite, yet Evie no longer tried to reach out when Jack became depressed. She no longer tried to reassure him. She no longer cared.

Jack became even more jealous and extreme in his reactions. He was desperate to win Evie back from the lover he created in his fantasies. And when she finally decided that the marriage was over, he vowed to fight whichever man had taken her from him.

Disgusted, Evie agreed to let him speak to the man who had destroyed their once-happy life together. She said she wouldn't tell him the man's name, but she would give him a photograph. He was someone they both knew, though she said she did not know him so well as she had once believed.

Jack desperately snatched the photograph from Evie's hand and looked at it. To his horror, it was a picture of himself.

Jack and Evie were among the lucky ones. They separated

without divorcing and both entered therapy. Neither is completely
healed of the past, but they are making enough progress so that
they are beginning to date again. They truly did have similar interests, and now that they are no longer trying to subvert their own
wants and needs for those of the other, their relationship is improv-
ing. They think they might get back together again, this time as
whole people. However, each knows that anything more than casual dating at this stage could cause a return to the addictive behavior that caused so much trauma. Thus, though their future is
uncertain, they may be among the lucky ones. Certainly they feel
there is enough of a chance to postpone completing the divorce
proceedings.

If Jack and Evie's experience is unusual, it is only because they
stand a chance of developing a new relationship based on mutual
interests, attraction, and respect. They are a couple who would
have been drawn to each other regardless of their pasts. Usually
however, two love-addicted people eventually break away from
each other when the less troubled of the two can no longer stand
the jealousy that accompanies all such relationships. Sooner or later
one of them comes to feel that the other is unhappy, seeking someone else, and otherwise destroying their love together.

Love addicts are insecure from the moment they fall in love
with each other. They are frightened by their happiness, terrified
that the other will leave them, and certain they are undeserving of
the intensity of the love they experience. Eventually, one of them
sabotages the relationship to such a degree that the other moves
on. Yet if that other becomes love-addicted to a healthy person, he
or she will then become the one who brings problems to the new
partnership.

Another Kind of Love Slave: Diane's Story
One of the difficulties in spotting the love-addicted individual is
that he or she often seems to be strong, in control; able to handle
any crisis. Sometimes this is seen in people whose actions we
honor, and sometimes it manifests itself in ways that society finds
repugnant. Since my primary work is in Manhattan, one of the most
densely populated cities in the world, I occasionally encounter

someone who has crossed over into the dark side of his or her existence in order to cope. Such a person is acting out in a manner where control has become extreme, and those who seek the person's services are users who have no desire for him or her to change in any way.

Diane seemed like any of a large number of bright, attractive, determined young women working to put themselves through college in New York. She had long blond hair, blue eyes, and a body that was obviously athletically shapely even under the conservative dress she wore when she entered my office. Her complexion was smooth and healthy, yet there was a hint of tiredness to her, as though life had not been easy despite her gifts of intellect and natural beauty. She seemed to be keeping herself in top condition so she could handle the rigors of a full course load, hours of studying, and enough hours of work so that she could pay room, board, and tuition. Had she been a waitress, a secretary, or a sales clerk, she would have been admired for her diligence and determination to make her way in the world. However, Diane earned her money in the shadow world of the soul. She was a dominatrix in a club where wealthy, powerful businessmen, athletes, and politicians paid large sums of money to be beaten and humiliated.

The acting out of the dark side of human existence is seen in every city of the world, and it comes in many forms.

In the private clubs like the one where Diane worked, any sexual perversion can be enjoyed in a safe, friendly atmosphere. The locations are expensive apartments and condominiums quietly converted and sound-proofed. The furnishings could be used as an example of understated elegance in *Architectural Digest*. There is music, a supply of expensive liquor, and beautiful, elegant women.

Then, when you are ready, you can go into a clean, well equipped private room in which to experience, for a few minutes or several hours, a physically safe taste of the horrors of the damned. For a steep price, a man can experience anything he desires.

In Diane's club, for example, all the paying members wished to be helpless and forced into experiences they carefully scripted in advance. Some wanted to be beaten. Others asked to be verbally humiliated while having to perform chores for their dominatrix (peeling, then feeding her grapes, washing her toes, or whatever).

The punishment requested was the man's special aphrodisiac, yet sexual intercourse was not allowed. The women were not pros-

titutes. Becoming erect while restrained then ordered to mastur-
bate himself was part of the humiliation and shame. Every part of
themselves and their sexual activity was "dirty," and no "nice" girl,
like the dominatrix, would wish to touch them "that way."

Diane was paid as much as $2,000 a week in salary and tips to
humiliate men who ran the kinds of businesses where she might
one day seek an entry level job. Her "working clothes" were high-
heeled black shoes, black stockings, and leather body wear de-
signed to make her look simultaneously sexual and hard. While
most of her clients were male, there were also women who sought
her attention. The women tended to want to be spanked with a riding crop. The men wanted to be struck in a variety of ways, at the
same time being verbally abused. They also wanted to be forced to
go on the floor on all fours, licking her feet, drinking from a bowl as
though they were dogs, and otherwise being humiliated.

Diane's world was as harshly contrasted as night and day. At
college she was a normal student, pursued by young men who ultimately thought of marriage, family, and the juggling of two careers.
She was learning about the workings of business, about art, science,
and history. She worked to master a foreign language. And she did
her homework in cheap cafés where no one minded the college students sitting for hours, sipping endless cups of coffee, eating whatever cheap food was available.

Yet when Diane went on the job, she entered a world of sophisticated violence, the fantasy equivalent of her own childhood.
The difference was that, as a child, she had not been the aggressor.
She had been a victim, enduring repeated beatings by her vicious
father in the small Midwest town where she grew up.

Diane did what many young girls do when their home life is
intolerable. She married the first young man who wanted her, focusing subconsciously on someone who had the same out-of-con-
trol temper as her father. It was not long after they were living
together that he beat her for the first time. By the third incident she
realized what was happening and fled, leaving her old life behind,
moving to New York, and enrolling in college.

Once again Diane became involved with a man, and once
again she chose the same type as her father. Certain that "all men
were alike" after the beatings, she told herself that it was impossible to have a "normal" relationship with a man. She took the job as
a dominatrix, sickened by the experience, angry, and focusing on

the high pay. She tolerated what she was doing by fantasizing that each man she humiliated was her father. Each man she struck was her father. Each man who paid to be allowed to grovel at her feet was her father.

As extreme as Diane's actions had become, she was really no different from love addicts who live in the suburbs, experiencing neither pain nor pleasure, leading lives of quiet desperation. She too was a love addict, as she found after taking the test you took in chapter 2.

What made Diane more extreme was that she had come to think that any sort of attention from her father was better than no attention. He was frequently absent from her life, on the job, drinking heavily in a bar until the early hours of the morning, or out with friends. He had to be close at hand to beat her. He had to be focused on her alone to beat her. The times of physical violence were as close to loving interaction as she ever experienced.

A puppet of her past, when Diane dated, she subconsciously sought young men who, though far more attentive than her father, were still violent. Being pushed around, humiliated, and beaten by them reminded her of love. And when she refused to be hurt any more, becoming the person who caused what amounted to fantasy pain to others, she was nevertheless continuing to act out a perverted love ritual.

Diane was not crazy, nor was she capable of becoming the female version of the stalker. She was a bright, beautiful young woman raised in a hellish home life, still seeking men in the manner of the frightened child. And fortunately, she wanted to flee the dark side of her existence.

Diane and I talked about her past. I had her remember the more vivid experiences of her childhood, thinking about what she had endured. She remembered her father's heavy drinking, the way he would become increasingly irritable in response to the alcohol. He was frequently in bar fights with other men, and the beatings she endured were not deliberate child abuse. If she spilled her milk when he was still sober, he would scold her and make her clean up the mess before getting more. If he had a few beers or several shots of whiskey in him, he would slap her, make her clean the mess, then spank her. His inhibitions and judgment were dulled by alcohol, and he violently overreacted.

Where was your mother in all this? I asked her, and again she looked at her childhood. She remembered that her mother encouraged her father, staying out of the way, watching his aggressiveness. She realized that her father's violent rages excited her mother. So long as she did not feel her husband's wrath, she was aroused by his aggressiveness. She liked to have sex with him after he had been in a bar fight. And she never seemed to think about the fact that her own daughter was being hurt when he exploded at home.

Diane's parents were obviously emotionally disturbed. The family was dysfunctional in ways that were exceedingly destructive for Diane. But she was also not truly loved by her parents. The only time she was really a part of the family was when she was the center of attention as her father struck her.

Diane worked the program in this book, coming to understand herself, her parents, and her childhood. She realized that she did not want to perpetuate the past. She did not want to spend her adult years acting out her childhood anger. And when she understood what had happened, she stopped looking upon men as though she had blinders on her eyes. She could see that the men she dated in the past drank too much, were regularly making comments that put others down, and had an angry way about them that was inappropriate for what was taking place in their lives.

A few months after Diane finished the program, she came by to tell me that she had met a new man, a young doctor who loved her and believed in her. He did not drink. He was not angry about life. And he respected her.

"I told him how I had put myself through school, and he just laughed. He thought it was funny. He was saddened by my past, and he did not like the fact that I thought I had to do that kind of work," Diane told me, happily. "But he told me to imagine what life might be like if he ever became chief of surgery and one of the other doctors' wives asked how we met. I could explain that we got together after I stopped earning a living by beating up men.

"It was funny, dark humor, Dr. Green, and I knew he meant for me to understand that he accepted me completely. He cares about my present and future, not my past. And what's most wonderful is that he has no illusions about himself, either. He told me that he spent so many years studying science that he really knows nothing about the arts except that he loves them. He delights in taking me to museums and art galleries where I can explain the stories of the artists and why something is considered unusual. He's as amazed that I respect his narrow education as I am that he respects who I am."

Diane's story was extreme. The controlled violence she acted out in the S&M club is not the usual. Yet her story does show to what depths self-hate can lead, when the pain of the past drives you to seek the same bitter patterns again and again. Once this is recognized, however, as Diane recognized her own problem, gaining self-respect and personal happiness is common. Resolving love addiction, as you will see, invariably results in a positive future previously unimaginable.

Do You Know Other Love Addicts?

Most love addicts involve themselves in lifestyles where no one casually observing them can imagine they are troubled. In fact, they may be among the most admired men and women you encounter. They seem like selfless individuals, always ready to sacrifice themselves for others.

This is because the love addict often feels responsible for the feelings of others. The love addict experiences a sense of guilt when someone close is troubled. Thus the love addict is likely to be the over-burdened volunteer, the organizer of office activities, church events, and the like. The love addict is the person who will intervene when someone is troubled, making suggestions for change, then becoming hurt or angry when the suggestions are not taken.

Sometimes the love addict is the always-harried volunteer, teaching Sunday School, organizing the office for the United Appeal, volunteering to bake cookies for a child's class, agreeing to work overtime, willing to take extra turns carpooling the children to Saturday classes, and otherwise becoming overly involved. Perpetually tired, harried, and determined to succeed, the love addict is often ineffectual with everything just because he or she is overburdened. Yet to admit to exhaustion is to admit to being imperfect.

"I can't let the church down." "I can't let my boss down." "The kids are counting on me." "Of course I'll help. I may be busy, but you know the saying, if you want something done right and on time, ask the busiest person around." These are the kinds of comments you hear from the love addict.

Other love addicts take an almost self-righteous attitude when, after offering a friend or acquaintance suggestions they are convinced will resolve a problem, they find that the suggestions are ignored. "I told you the Prentice account wasn't worth saving. I said you shouldn't waste your time with a lost cause when there is more important business to handle." "I told Sharon that Bill was no good for her, but would she listen? Now she's heartbroken and all because she didn't take my advice. Well, I can't keep feeling responsible. I tried. I really did. She just had to do things her way." And on and on.

You know the type. All-knowing, announcing to the world that when someone does not do what he or she suggests, the consequences are out of control. The person often seems self-centered and self-righteous, a know-it-all who will tear someone else down in order to build up his or her own self-esteem. Yet the love addict exhibiting this behavior is actually quite insecure. Behind the attacks is the belief that, when something goes wrong, there is a personal responsibility. Making it clear to others that he or she tried to do the "right" thing and that the other person acted differently exonerates the love addict of guilt.

In a relationship, the same attitude may manifest itself in other ways. "I followed the recipe exactly, so if you don't like the dinner, blame the author of the cookbook." (Or your mother. Or whatever the source of the recipe might be.) "I told you to dress warmly. Now you've got a cold and it's all your fault."

Or there may be a self-deprecating attitude, such as, "I should have warned you about putting gas in your car. I didn't know how much driving you were doing, but I should have thought to remind you." "If I hadn't suggested we watch that movie, you would have gotten to bed earlier last night and been more productive at the office. Then you wouldn't have had to work overtime." Or even such an extreme as, "Sometimes one person can make a difference. I should have signed the petition requesting Iraq peacefully withdraw from Kuwait. Maybe if I had added my name to the list, our young people wouldn't have had to fight in the Gulf War."

There is an exaggerated sense of responsibility that carries over into the relationship. If a woman cries during a particularly sad movie, the love-addicted male is likely to apologize for whatever it was he did to cause his beloved to be upset. If a man has indigestion after eating in a restaurant, the love-addicted woman may vow to take cooking lessons so she causes him no further discomfort.

Sometimes the love addict appears to be generous. He or she may loan the love object a car, taking inconvenient public transportation. Behind this seeming act of kindness is the truth that the love addict inwardly feels a little responsible for the fact that the other person's engine wouldn't start.

The love addict is the kind of friend who will worry if you don't telephone periodically, then worry when you do. "I'm taking so much of your valuable time." Again, it all goes back to childhood, to the time when there was a desperate, yet inevitably unsuccessful effort to please an undemonstrative, possibly uncaring, absentee, or dead parent. But instead of looking at the past, the love addict merely reacts to it. It is as though the worries of childhood that come from lacking the experience to be an objective observer of life continue to dominate the adult's thought process. You may be an executive in charge of a large office staff, functioning flawlessly on the job. But deep in your heart, when faced with an intimate relationship, you have the insecurities of a five-year-old, hiding under the covers, terrified of the dark.

Understanding Your Own History

If you are like most love addicts, you may cling to a bad relationship partly out of the fear of being without that relationship. When I say "bad" I do not mean you are necessarily being abused in some way. Being involved with a man or woman who is physically or, more commonly, verbally abusive is an obvious problem. Everyone recognizes that something is wrong with such a relationship. But a relationship can be "bad" for a number of other, far more common reasons that are readily overlooked. For example, suppose it is obvious that the person you feel you cannot live without, the person to whom you emotionally cling, has no interest in you. You are ignored, or perhaps the person has made very clear that you are one of several people the person is dating; yet you "know" that if you are monogamous, the loved one will ultimately choose you. You are constantly disappointed that the intensity of your feelings is not returned.

Or perhaps you are living together without passion. There is no real intimacy, neither physical nor in the way you interact. You might as well be roommates linked by a service, two people leading separate lives yet sharing a common living space.

Whatever the circumstances, you tell yourself that everything is fine. You try harder. You endure. You suppress your emotions or overreact, always smiling, always supportive, always ready to do whatever the loved one desires, even if it conflicts with your own long-held plans. And if this is the healthiest relationship you have ever had, you may cling even harder. After all, everything else you have known is worse. It is better to place expectations on neutral than to endure the destructiveness you have experienced with others.

The problem is that you deserve better than you have. The relationship is a bad one because it is limiting. You can never be a whole person with your love object. You are never in a position where you can grow together.

Thus, "bad" does not mean violence. "Bad" does not mean that you are being verbally abused, mocked, or otherwise treated as less than a whole person. You are simply denying yourself the full range of emotional and interpersonal experience that is the right, the joy, and the potential of every man or woman.

If you are like many men and women, you cling to a bad relationship because you know you will feel frightened without it. If you feel this way, you need to ask yourself, "What is this fear? Where does it come from?"

When you allow yourself to think about it, you will find that it is based on childhood feelings of being helpless, inadequate, too small, unloved, and unwanted. Those feelings might have formed an accurate perception of your world as a four-year-old, especially if your parents were not good at helping you develop confidence in yourself and your abilities. But that perception is not an accurate one today when you are an adult. You have to orient yourself to the reality that you are now capable of coping independently with life.

So why are you having problems? It is because you are not recognizing who you are today, what your capabilities as an adult happen to be. Instead, you are living your life dependent upon a person—the image of a parent, often—who is repeating the same pattern of undermining or failing to support your strengths and self-worth. Only now that "person" is internalized as self-criticism.

It is important to analyze your pattern of relationships to see whether something destructive is being repeated. Ask yourself whether there have been similarities in your love relationships. What are the similarities among the traits that you find most appealing, and what are the similarities among the traits you find most distressing? And what about the patterns of interaction? Who's more open? Who's more often in control of when and how you spend your time together? Who seems more in love and committed?

Which needs of yours were most fulfilled in past relationships? Which were the most disappointed?

How did past relationships end? Who ended them and why? What feelings were you left with?

If you are in a bad relationship, are the attachments of the past similar in traits and behavior to the one you now feel you probably should end? As a love addict, you will see that a self-defeating pattern is being repeated in each of your relationships.

It is important to understand that not all aspects of your emotional drives are bad ones. They are just based on past thoughts, feelings, and beliefs rather than an understanding of your current situation.

For example, there was Zena, a young woman in her late twenties who was constantly getting involved with abusive men. "They're aggressive," she told me, a little embarrassed. "I like that. I've always wanted to be raped by a man I liked."

I was surprised until Zena explained she was not talking about actually being raped. "That's a horribly violent act," said Zena. "No woman wants to experience something like that. I'm talking about the game of rape where the man I love overpowers me in the bedroom, in the living room, or anywhere else he wants me when we're alone together and in the mood for sex."

There was nothing odd about Zena's fantasy, and perhaps that was one of the reasons she avoided looking at other aspects of her relationships. Researchers ranging from Nancy Friday to the Kinsey Institute to the staff of *Redbook* and other publications have all found rape fantasies popular among men and women. In healthy relationships, there are sex games where one person overpowers the other, sometimes holding the lover down during foreplay and intercourse, sometimes tying him to the bed or restraining him in some other manner. The man and the woman often take turns being "the victim," each playing a dominant role from time to time. The "victim" may request restraints secure enough to truly be helpless, or know that the bonds are so loose he or she can slip out at any time.

No matter how the game is played, the couple know their limits. Both enjoy playing. Neither is hurt. And neither is ever really out of control.

Psychologists studying the loving side of sex games have found that there are a number of reasons why rape fantasies are popular. One that seemed to fit Zena was the idea of being wanted.

The "victim" sees the partner not as oppressively dominant but as being overwhelmed with desire. No matter how rough the day has been, no matter what problems have been faced, it is obvious from playing out the fantasy that the aggressor loves and desires the partner. And since most rape fantasy players alternate regularly, the game is a way for each to reinforce awareness of the other's love in a playful manner.

Zena began talking about her childhood. Her father had been a cold, distant man. Her parents had six children when he decided they had enough. He was a factory worker who had to take all the overtime he could get to feed and clothe his family. The only time there was any money for personal pleasure was when his wife could take a part-time job. Yet with the babies born close together, they both realized that nothing much would change until the youngest was in school.

Zena had been the accidental baby, the seventh child, born when her father felt overwhelmed by financial responsibilities. Furious, he refused to try to bond with Zena. She was not a new life to be loved and nurtured, in his mind. Instead, she was an unwanted nuisance, the last straw in his fight to keep the family at a level higher than mere subsistence. Zena meant he would always be working two jobs, even when his wife could return to working. Zena's birth meant that he would not be able to save for his retirement. Zena meant that hobbies could not be indulged, a larger home would probably be too expensive for what he earned, that debt would be a way of life.

There was nothing wrong with Zena. She was a happy baby, healthy, a child any parent would love—if he let himself. Zena's father did not.

Not that Zena ever understood all these dynamics. How could she? Her father refused to deal with the fact that his real frustration was with himself. He saw himself as a failed provider, a man who was somehow less of a person than he believed he should be. His parents had had both a large family and money for extras. Of course, he ignored the fact that his mother was a clothing piece worker from their home, and that his sisters had had to work the moment they were old enough to help. He ignored the fact that his father, a laborer in a steel mill, was slightly disabled in an accident, resulting in an insurance payment that helped them move into a better neighborhood. And he also ignored the fact that he himself had worked in the mill after dropping out of high school.

He conveniently forgot that when Zena came along, he and his wife owned two well-used but serviceable cars, a television set, and a record player, all luxuries his parents had never had. His father took the streetcar, and the only radio they owned for many years was a crystal set he had made himself.

Zena was a victim who never understood what had happened. In hindsight, as an adult scanning her past, she was able to see her childhood in a different perspective. But Zena had been a woman convinced that she was no good, that she was unworthy of love, that no man would ever intensely want her. Thus the rape fantasy was nothing more than a game to prove to herself that some man would find her worth pursuing.

Unfortunately, Zena picked the males she dated with her childhood emotions firmly in control. She saw male aggression as loving commitment. Instead of seeking loving males with whom she could explore all aspects of life, including physical intimacy, she was drawn to men who were angry, their aggression directed at life in general. As a result, she never found the happiness she expected.

This pattern of failed relationships with the same kind of person is a major clue not only to love addiction but to the need to review your childhood. The healthy adult may have problems. The healthy adult may have one or more failed relationships. But because the healthy adult recognizes personal control, he or she will take the time to review the recently failed relationship. The healthy adult will analyze what went well, what went wrong, and why. And with the next partner, sure enough, things will be different. If there are problems, they will be new ones based on their distinct personalities, not phantoms from childhood. And if the relationship is successful, as so many of them are, it will be because destructive actions have been eliminated as much as possible.

So the past is the key to a pattern of problem relationships. The love addict is simply repeating what amounts to unfinished, unresolved childhood experience.

One of my patients, a woman named Susan, had parents who were constantly depressed when she was growing up. Susan never knew the reason for their depression, and practically speaking it did not matter. Perhaps there were clinical problems. Perhaps there was a bad marriage. All Susan knew was that she felt responsible for ending the depression as a child. She got good grades in school, not because she had any direction but because she hoped they would please her parents. She cleaned her room, learned to fix their favorite dinners, and even bought the clothing styles she thought they would enjoy, although she didn't always like them.

As an adult, Susan repeated the pattern. Each of her serious relationships was with a male who was depressed. Some people seeking a pet are drawn to the runt of the litter. Or they will see several kittens in a cage and choose the one that seems to be helpless and picked on by the others. Susan would enter a room and be drawn to the lonely man off in a corner looking sad, obviously failing in the effort to force himself to have a good time.

With each new relationship, Susan decided that she was going to be the person who cured the man's depression. She failed every time. She did not realize that only the person who is depressed can change his or her emotions. Instead, when she failed, as was inevitable with anyone who does not wish to change, she became depressed herself. Then she became frustrated. Finally she decided it was time to move on to the next relationship, invariably with a depressed man she was determined to cure.

I had Susan take the same test you took in chapter 2. The results were not surprising.

Susan answered "yes" to the question about low self-esteem. She did not look to others to make her happy, but she looked to the *moods* of others to make her happy. That was a slight difference from what many love slaves experience. She was happy if the other person was happy. She was troubled if the other person was unhappy. Eventually she handled his continuing depression by getting rid of the relationship and seeking another that was essentially the same.

Susan said that she needed a *happy* man to make her life fulfilled. But she did not want a man who was happy. She wanted a depressed man who was changed to a happy man by her efforts.

Susan was obsessive. She needed constant assurance about the relationship, though that assurance could only come from mood changes. She was never turned on by someone who was happy and interested in her. She was only drawn to the man who became happy as a result of the relationship. That was why she had to begin with a man who was depressed.

The questions on the love addiction test kept being answered positively. She feared loneliness. She was possessive, envious, and jealous. Her hopes and dreams were projected onto her love object. She always placed the man on a pedestal. She also found that her sexual desire came when the man was losing his depression, not when he remained depressed. Again her relationship was with a changing mood, not a flesh-and-blood human being.

Susan said she always abandoned her individuality for her love object, determined to stop his depression. She would buy clothing she thought would make the man happy. She would take him to movies, to the theater, to concerts. She would go with him for long walks in the park, or she would go looking at the art for sale in inner-city galleries. She would adapt her schedule to his so they could have sex whenever he might want it. Yet if nothing seemed to work to draw him out of his depression, she would become frustrated. She would stop being adaptable, loving, and caring. "I'd just tune him out," she told me, and that was when she was ready to move on to the next man.

Susan also talked of hungering for closeness to her parents. She said that she perceived herself as being uncared for as a child. She also felt dependent upon others for her sense of self-worth and well being.

The list continued. Although she was not self-destructive in her personal habits, using neither drugs nor alcohol, her health was not always good. Her immune system seemed low and she admitted that she was plagued by colds, flu, and other minor ailments throughout the year.

Susan was the classic love slave, the puppet of her past. In fact, she tried to say that being a love slave was good for her. It meant she was caring, giving, selfless. "I'm trying to make my depressed lovers smile," she told me. But once Susan scanned her past relationships as part of the program, she realized what she had been doing. Her problem was not with being attractive, having self-worth, or being of value. She was trying to correct her "failings" as a child. She could not stop her parents' depression, so she sought her parents in the form of each new depressed man in her life. It was then that she learned to cut the strings, to free herself from the marionette master of her childhood, to heal.

For two years she concentrated on her job, keeping her friendships with men extremely casual. Eventually she began dating, making certain that the relationships were constructive, each respecting the other, neither trying to dominate. One man seemed especially attractive, and after several months of dating, she realized she loved him and he loved her. Today they are happily married, Susan having two children, the couple sharing in both parenting and their respective careers. They are a team, coming together from love, not manipulative needs.

Why did it take so long? Part of the answer lies in the society in which we live. In the next chapter I would like to take a closer look at the many ways in which our culture accepts, celebrates, and encourages the unhealthy feelings and behavior known as love addiction.

Chapter 5

The Love Slave and Society

It has long been difficult for the love addict to heal because contemporary culture has glorified the obsessed lover as a positive relationship role model. Popular music, for example, has songs glorifying what often is obsessive love with words such as: "Hopelessly devoted to you." "True love." "Forever." "Till the end of time." "Always."

In the late 1980s and early 1990s, a number of popular films, such as *Ghost*, explored the idea of love lasting beyond the grave. Such movies, though they often ended with the living character finding happiness with someone still alive, glorified the intensity of a love so great that the beloved was protected after the lover's death.

While there is a negative side to obsessive love, it is seldom the focus of stories other than those found in religious settings. For example, there is the Biblical story of Adam and Eve. While this story is important on several levels—the issue of disobedience towards God and its consequences for humanity being the primary one—it is also a story of love addiction. Adam and Eve so focus on each other that they act in a manner that ultimately causes their destruction. It is not until the positive loving relationship of Abraham and Sarah that there is a full healing with the Creator. And Abraham's healthy love so heals that he becomes one of the most important early religious leaders mentioned in the Old Testament, the New Testament, and the Koran.

The Pygmalion myth deals with a man obsessively in love with the image of a woman and her willingness to be transformed. While the play of the same name by George Bernard Shaw ends tragically for the hero, Professor Higgins, audiences wanted the obsessed lover to triumph. They wanted to see the love object effectively seduced, and so the ending was changed for the play and movie *My Fair Lady*. Instead of the transformed Eliza Doolittle marrying Freddy, a man who is in love with the whole woman (*Pyg-*

malion), she returns to Professor Higgins, embracing a man who is truly a love slave (*My Fair Lady*).

Cultures not sharing the Judeo/Christian heritage often focused on the positive side of love addiction. In Greek and Roman mythology, for example, there were stories of love between gods and mortals so intense that a god might give up immortality or a mortal might be raised to the level of a deity. Early literature also had stories such as the one Homer wrote of Paris following his beloved, Helen of Troy, to what seemed the ends of the world. More modern myths have been used in movies where enchanted statues and mannequins come alive because of the love of a mortal store employee or other individual (*One Touch of Venus; Mannequin;* etc.).

Prince Charming knew no more of Cinderella than that she was beautiful, danced divinely, and was light enough on her feet so as not to break her glass slipper. Yet he because so obsessed with the fantasy image that he was willing to turn the kingdom upside down in order to find him.

And what of the Handsome Prince who awakened Sleeping Beauty from her slumber? No doubt she had morning breath as foul as a dragon's mouth, and yet he could not live without her.

How do children's books end? Frequently with the words, "And they lived happily ever after." The total commitment of one person to another has long meant happiness. Love so strong that the lover never strays even in thoughts has long been the idealized lifestyle.

Escapist literature, such as romance novels, frequently glorify commitment "forever" following what is really a superficial short-term relationship, albeit an emotionally intense one. "Forever" love at first sight is real in many of the stories. And when there is seemingly no love, when there is nothing but surface anger, disdain, or hostility between the heroine and the primary man in her life, the reader knows that the emotions will change to love. There is chemistry. There is magic. There is unswerving commitment.

If you have ever read such a book, you know you will never see a scene where a non-love slave says to her beloved: "You know, Reginald, we really hardly know each other. My horse went wild while I was riding across Pommsley Terrace as a guest of Lord Pimpleface and you happened to hear my screams for help. I was impressed with your powerful physique when you ran across hill and dale, field and stream, until you caught up with my stallion and brought him to a halt. Then you took me in your powerful arms and carried me ten miles to Pommsley Manor.

"We have shared some unusual experiences, Reginald, not the least of which was discovering that you are the third Earl of Rutabaga, once removed, and heir to the Rutabaga millions. Not to mention the fact that you are a very good chaste kisser who sets my heart afire without laying a hand on my bosom or otherwise taking liberty with me.

"But physical lust does not a relationship make, Reginald. I think we should take some time getting to know each other. We should share our hopes, our dreams, an exploration of our mutual careers, perhaps having premarital counseling. Then, if we seem compatible for reasons other than sensual desire, we can become engaged."

No book will provide such a harsh dose of reality at the end, yet love addicts often use escapist fiction to justify their actions. The negative side of love addiction, the side that assures a failed relationship over time, is portrayed as the start of a positive relationship in many books of fiction.

This is why a love addict will remain in what is recognized as a bad relationship. It is not the quality of that relationship. It is the fact that it exists at all that matters. And in our society, image is more important than substance.

Take a look at the magazines meant for single men and women, as well as many of the more sophisticated magazines for teenaged girls. These publications regularly tell how to attract a lover, how to keep the person happy, how to keep the person from straying. The reader learns that the more involved with the process of establishing a relationship he or she can be, the greater the chance for success. In the 1960s, Helen Gurley Brown's pioneering book *Sex and the Single Girl* made it very clear that with determination and a change in attitude, every young woman can find happiness. She will have the career she desires, and more importantly, she will have the man she seeks.

Magazines such as *Cosmopolitan* have long stressed the idea that determination can assure success. They reinforce the love slave's idea that he or she must hold on to the object of attention if only by fingernails being slowly ripped from one's fingers. It is only when love addiction crosses the line into mental illness, when determination becomes stalking, that we criticize what we otherwise glorify.

In the 1950s, as society was going through transition, many college students said that the males were there to get an education, and the females were in class to get their "Mrs." degree. The pursuit of the man was the primary goal of "good girls" who did well in school, dressed conservatively, remained virgins, and saw marriage and family as the ultimate achievement in life. Even publications such as the new *Playboy,* which was dedicated to a hedonistic male lifestyle, still paid tribute to the stereotype. The centerfold was frequently the girl next door, and though she was sold as a lust object, it was made clear that one, and only one male would ever possess her.

Working with media critic and author Daphne Davis, I took a look at some of the better known influences within popular culture. These all deal with love slaves, the addicted, obsessive lover.

For example, an attractive young college student, majoring in communication, was found to have worked her way through school as a prostitute in Las Vegas. She was selective about her men and well paid. After leaving this life and working the program in this book, she came to realize that her father had been coldly undemonstrative when she was growing up. Each time a man wanted her, was willing to go so far as to pay money to be with her, she became sexually aroused. She was receiving the love she had been denied. It was a fleeting experience, physically dangerous, and psychologically destructive. Yet it worked. Similarly obsessive characters, like many of those portrayed by Ava Gardner, though often misunderstood, are actually quite realistic.

Gardner epitomized the nymphomaniac or "love junkie" in the movies *The Barefoot Contessa* and *The Sun Also Rises.* These were very much characters involved with love addiction. Some women and men use sex, either in a monogamous relationship or as a regular part of even fairly casual dating, to feel loved. They will have sex with anyone, not because they have insatiable sexual appetites but because the physical attention is a way of feeling wanted.

There have been numerous others. *Looking for Mr. Goodbar* had a woman haunting singles bars in order to find love through casual, dangerous sex. The novel and movie were based on a love addicted woman's murder chronicled in the book *Closing Time.*

The book *9½ Weeks* is the story of a man who thrives on women who fall in love with his image, then become so sexually addicted that they will tolerate physical and psychological abuse.

Fatal Attraction has a love addict turn stalker after she misreads the intention of a married lover with whom she has a brief affair. *The Postman Always Rings Twice* tells of the intense affair between a drifter and an immigrant's wife. Their relationship is extreme enough to end with the murder of the woman's husband.

The protagonists in some of the novels by Danielle Steele, Sidney Sheldon, Jackie Collins, Harold Robbins, and Judith Krantz are often love addicted. However, frequently the books end while the relationship is still thriving. Thus the love addiction is viewed as positive.

There are numerous classics, of course. *Anna Karenina* was Leo Tolstoy's account of a woman's obsessive relationship with a Russian Count. And Vladimir Nabokov's *Lolita* deals with a middle-aged man's obsessive relationship with a nubile young girl. Both, in effect, are tragedies, yet there is sensitivity towards the love addict, as though there, for the grace of God, could be any one of us.

One of the most successful movies about love addiction, and later one of the most watched movies ever produced, is the classic story *Gone with the Wind* in which the heroine, Scarlett O'Hara, was denied both her father's love and that of Ashley Wilkes. Then Rhett Butler, who pursues her, never is quite able to possess Scarlett because her fantasies of Ashley destroy any chance for happiness or sexual fulfillment with Rhett.

The intensely sexual *Last Tango In Paris* was notable for actor Marlon Brando's monologues about his unhappy childhood, estrangement from his parents, and bitter, failed relationships with women. The action in the movie, exhibitionistic sexual trysts in a Paris apartment, was typical of the love addict.

Somerset Maugham's story *The Pool* is the story of a love addict who marries a Tahitian woman who truly loves him. However, when she realizes that he is only seeing her as a fantasy, she has an affair with a fat German man, far less attractive than her husband. For a moment he sees her in a negative light, physically striking her. The woman is delighted, not because she likes violence but because perhaps their relationship can be saved, perhaps he truly can accept her for herself. However, the violence is shameful to him and he feels terrible that he struck his love object. She once again becomes miserable, and he, misunderstanding the relationship, commits suicide.

Maugham's *Of Human Bondage* is a book the author claimed was partly autobiographical, revealing his own troubled youth and search for love. The story tells of the student Philip Carey's obsession with waitress Mildred Rogers, who disdained him and sought a wealthy man to be her husband. Carey developed an all-consuming love/hate relationship with the woman. He willingly cared for her when she was abandoned by her love, a married man, who made her pregnant. Then, after leaving the hospital, she had an affair with Carey's best friend. Still he took her back after the friend dumped her. Eventually, though, Carey falls in love with another woman for mature reasons, and realizes that his obsession with the waitress had to do with his own troubled past. After healing, he marries the woman who looked upon him as an equal, not someone who could be manipulated as Mildred had done.

Among the other works dealing with the theme are D.H. Lawrence's *Women In Love* and *Lady Chatterly's Lover*, and *The Alexandria Quartet* by Lawrence Durell. The latter is a series of four novels—*Justine*; *Bathazar*; *Mountolive*; and *Clea*. The stories are similar ones, following a woman named Justine through a series of relationships. Both she and the men in her life are all love addicted. Justine delights in being whatever the man desires, a dressmaker's dummy on which the men hang their fantasies, loving her for what they want her to be, never knowing what she is.

Justine survives by making demands on the men as proof of their love. She receives physical gifts, but she also robs them of their life's blood, always with their consent. Each feeds off the other, and by the end of the four novels, all the players have suffered. However, along the way they have so much fun together acting out their fantasies that the novels have been used by several of my patients to justify their own addiction. Prior to seeking help, they ignored the endings and looked at the pleasures along the way, emulating a fantasy life that ultimately was destructive for them as well.

Romance writers and many of the influential creators of popular culture are unlikely to ever do the public the favor of taking reality into account, and so it is small surprise that many love addicts use escapist fiction to justify their actions. The negative side of love addiction, the side that assures a failed relationship over time, is portrayed as the start of a positive relationship by the authors they like the best.

This is an important reason why a love addict will remain in what he or she knows to be a bad relationship. It is not the quality of that relationship but the fact that it exists at all that matters. After all, in our society image is more important than substance.

Part of society's message, actually, is based on healthy fears. AIDS and other sexually transmitted diseases have put an end to the 1960s ethic of free love, effectively re-elevating monogamy to its former privileged status. AIDS has given many healthy people, as well as love addicts, a powerful motivation to stay in one relationship—even though that relationship may be a troubled one. It is yet another way in which we tell love addicts, "Nothing's wrong."

A Taste of Reality

Sometimes the life of a love addict may indeed resemble fiction—but not the kind of fiction he may wish it to. Not long ago I happened to read *Command And I Will Obey You*, by the Italian novelist Albert Moravia. The story concerns a love addict who willingly goes along with whatever his wife desires. Each day he cleans the house while she, dressed only in high heels, nylons, a bra, and panties, stands over him. This arouses him, because he is a masochist, and she for her part enjoys dominating him.

The hero of Moravia's novel literally does everything for his wife. He works in an office. He supports the family. At home he fixes their meals as well as scrubbing the floors and walls daily and handling any other chores that need to be done. He does not care that she fails to share the work with him. He is pleased with her growing cruelty, thriving on the disdain he obviously feels for himself as well.

Ultimately the hero's wife engages in the ultimate cruelty, ordering him to pack her bags so she can leave home with her boyfriend. He obeys her, placing the bags in the trunk, then finally becomes so irate that he shoots her as she starts to leave with her lover.

Only a couple of weeks after I read this novel, one of my patients told me of his own obsessive addiction to a demanding, uncaring woman. Carl was a wealthy, masochistic developer whose love object was a physical fitness instructor he had met in a martial arts class. He was drawn to her beauty and haughtiness; she was delighted by his money and his willingness to do literally anything for her.

The relationship they acted out together was remarkably similar to that portrayed in the novel. She too wore minimal, sensual clothing, while he handled all domestic chores, after which they had sex. The sex was quite pleasant for him, but she took things a step further. Recognizing his emotional weakness, she convinced him that he could only sustain an erection with her. She caused him to believe that he could find happiness with no other woman. She made him feel that the only pleasure he would find in life was through her, and if he did not do as she desired, she would leave him.

Carl was given a list of "presents" that would be required to keep her happy. These ranged from an emerald necklace to a Mercedes-Benz coupe, all of which he bought her. She was given her own American Express Card and a bank account with a liberal "allowance" larger than most people's annual incomes. She spent most of her time lazing around her apartment.

Carl's wealth was mostly inherited, so he was spending increasing amounts of time taking care of his beloved. She eventually tired of the sport, however, and one day she ordered him to pack her suitcases for her. She had decided to run off and have an affair with a professional trainer.

Carl recognized that he could not physically compete with the handsome lover. Though he did not draw a gun and shoot her, he was genuinely shocked that she would not want to stay with a man who so adored her that he would lavish her with possessions. What had gone wrong? Curiously, Carl's lover turned out to have more sense than greed. She had come to feel that she could not tolerate a man who did not love her. She told him that he only loved his image of her. He did not care for her as a person. He had no interest in encouraging or supporting her life. He wanted to love a fantasy, not a whole person. She explained to Carl that at least her boyfriend loved her for herself.

At that point, as in Moravia's book, Carl started to become violent. He raised his fists in anger, forgetting that they had met in a martial arts class, where she was a senior student. She beat him up, leaving him with a dislocated shoulder, called the hospital for him, then ran off with the boyfriend.

Not long after this Carl took the test from chapter 2, answering "yes" to every question. He was a complete love addict, though this was where life was better than fiction. He worked the program, revealing the fact that his father was a workaholic. The few times father and son interacted were when his father beat him, something that occurred with every infraction of family rules. Since the only time Carl was involved with his father was when he was being punished, he began equating love and pain.

Carl's mother was constantly depressed. She went to see a therapist four or five days a week, constantly becoming introspective and uncaring about her family. She declared all aspects of her life to be psychologically significant, and was unable to respond to her son in a normal way. Even a simple question such as his asking her what he should make for dinner became a puzzle for her. She worried that there was a hidden message, that he was sexually attracted to her—a ridiculous conclusion unrelated to the truth. Then she would go to her analyst and compare Carl's question about the meal with her own desire for her father, her self-declared penis envy, and other feelings. She was clearly disturbed, the therapist was less than competent, and eventually Carl's mother had to be hospitalized. She later died young, of lung cancer from chain smoking from the time she was a teenager.

Carl's father then put even more time into work. The end result was a child who felt deprived of love, of warmth, of all that he needed for nurturing. But Carl, at least, was lucky. He eventually healed.

If this is the reality of love addiction, then why don't we see it more often? What fascinates us about the love slaves of song, movie, and romance? The truth is, there is something exciting about being the object of obsessive love. We don't think of the negative. We think of an erotic existence where lust overcomes rational reasoning. We often place our fantasies into such situations. One man may delight in the image of a woman running him down, tying him to a bed, stripping off his clothes, and having repeated sex with him. A woman may fantasize a lover who seduces her by repeatedly catering to her every whim, plying her with the sensual experiences of fine wine, elaborately prepared gourmet food, flowers, candy, and perfume. Whatever the case, the commitment is always viewed as total, the acting out of every fantasy ever created.

Yet it cannot be denied that although we may enjoy escapist entertainment, real life requires a more mature approach to relationships. Only the immature person will look at such fiction and think it would be healthy. Humans are meant to enjoy committed intimacy. Once chemical lust yields to true awareness, we become far happier in our interpersonal relationships. Sex often becomes slower, more sensual, the delight coming from the whole person and not just the mutual physical arousal. Foreplay may begin with a deep conversation about a matter of mutual interest and concern. Then, as each respects the other's statements, there is a glow of happiness from the knowledge of having this friend. From that may come a fresh look into the lover's heart, a touch, a kiss, and a gradual movement into sexual intimacy. But instead of a physical release from the genital tension of lust, the sex act becomes a celebration of full love. Those who have known a mature love recognize that the fictional glorification of love addiction, though fun to read or see, offers no long-term satisfaction when compared to mature commitment.

Love: The Love Slave's Drug of Choice

The love slave, of course, does not know this. And society's toleration of, indeed approval of, the experience of love addiction does him a sad disservice. Love addiction, for all it may seem glamorous or noble, is in reality as deadly as any other form of addiction. In fact, as far back as the writing of Sigmund Freud, love addiction has been recognized to be a form of escape as destructive as opiates and alcohol.

There is a natural tendency for people to resist the idea that a human relationship can be psychologically equivalent to drug addiction. We worry not about those who are slaves to love but about the loners in society—people who cannot relate to other people. The idea that someone must constantly be involved with others is seen either as positive or as a less-than-serious problem. Yet evidence is growing that it is very serious indeed. Of this evidence, perhaps most telling is the fact, as psychologists have found, that drug and alcohol addiction often occurs among adults whose early emotional needs were not met—the same difficulties experienced by love addicts. Simply put, drugs are a substitute for human ties. Everyone knows people who replace romantic relationships with other forms of escape, such as alcohol and drugs. Sometimes this is a periodic escape, with the use or abuse of such substances taking place between love affairs. We accept as "normal" the man or woman sitting in a corner of a bar, drinking steadily, trying to forget Sam or Sheila, Greg or Ginny, or whoever else has just left them. Of course, we expect the person to come around eventually, to try again, to heal. But interim drug abuse is acceptable, even though it is a way of avoiding having to confront past relationship problems and future relationship opportunities.

Not many people realized in the past the extent to which love relationships too can be an addiction. This was because psychologists and others were looking at all relationships involving two living, breathing, "whole" individuals as healthy. They assumed that the appearance of the couple also reflected the reality of the couple. They did not realize that the love addict is romancing a fantasy placed on a whole individual he or she does not try to know as a person. In reality the love object is as much an escape as drugs or alcohol, but the appearance of the relationship is more socially acceptable.

That the love addict is not involved with a "real" person is especially important to remember. Certainly the love object is a living, breathing, unique individual. He or she has thoughts, feelings, desires, hopes, and dreams. Yet to the love slave the love object is little more than a paper doll on which to hang the fantasies formed by the past. All relationships are treated identically. Each new man or woman is uniquely different from the previous one, yet the fantasy that the love slave uses to adorn the relationship is the same. And this routine action of the love-addicted personality means that each relationship is being used, not enjoyed.

Some people are addicted to tranquilizers. They tell themselves they cannot have peace without another dose. They tell themselves that they lack the power within to find ways to cope with stress. They tell themselves that they are not capable of relaxing in a way others find normal. Their need is the achievement of peace of mind, an internal action, not one that comes from external substances or other people.

The love object is simply the drug of choice for the love addict. The thought processes of the love addict and the drug addict are the same. The love slave is saying that healing the past is impossible without the beloved of the moment; in this way he avoids the inner strengths that low self-esteem has prevented him from seeing. Of course, there is something else he is not seeing, and that is the love object him- or herself. The love slave might just as well be having sex with a sophisticated version of the inflatable dolls sold in disreputable stores. The love object is no more than a human opiate when viewed through the subconscious mind of the love slave.

An Escape from Pain

Sigmund Freud saw close parallels between being in love and hypnosis. A person's self-love, he noted, can be transferred from the individual's own ego to another person, with the other gaining increasing possession of what should be the self-love of the lover's ego. There is a surrendering of the self, the ego, to the object of the lover's desire. This results in the lover's ego being impoverished—a healthy step toward bonding in a normal relationship but an action that further destroys the love slave's already-low sense of self.

Freud pointed out that in hypnosis, the subject focuses solely on the hypnotist, voluntarily surrendering his or her will so as to be able to accept suggestions. There is almost a complete absence of critical thinking. Whatever is suggested by the hypnotist will almost always be followed by the subject. It is just the same with the infatuated lover; during this early stage of the relationship, there is the same sapping of the will. The lover wants to please the love object. The lover is focused entirely on the love object. The lover receives almost all gratification from the reactions of the love object.

Love is the ideal vehicle for addiction because it can exclusively claim the person's consciousness, shutting out pain. Addictions are, at least in the early period of abusive use, both reassuring and all-consuming. The drug addict snorts, swallows, or injects whatever brings emotional peace and an escape from the perceived pressures all around. For a brief time personal problems are masked beyond recognition by the highs and lows of drug addiction. There is no true pleasure, none of the natural high that comes from having a positive experience when making yourself vulnerable to another person. But there is also no pain, and it is the absence of pain that helps reinforce the drug addict.

It is no different for the love slave. No different, except that the love slave has society to cheer him on. Having an emotionally intimate relationship is good, he is constantly being told. (Can you imagine a drug user being congratulated in this way?) Society usually accepts that love will be all-consuming, at least in the early stages of that relationship. "Of course Geraldine made a mistake on the Harrison account. She's in love." "Stan missed another appointment this week, but everyone's understanding. They know about his relationship with Julie and are thrilled that he's found love at last."

The drug addict or alcoholic typically avoids having to face the destructive side of his dependency, and so it is with the love addict. The drug addict uses the drug of choice to control his or her life; the love addict uses the image, the fantasy, of the love object. When a love slave seeks a commitment to another person with the unconscious intention of filling a void, the object quickly becomes the center of her life. This is like the teenager who becomes pregnant, then moves in with her boyfriend, as a way of being able to leave an intolerable home environment. The real problems, not only with the family relationship but also with the responsibility being created through the pregnancy, are not faced. If you are still hurting from the unfulfilled needs of childhood, and if you convince yourself that your love object can heal you, he or she becomes all-consuming. You will do anything to keep that person happy. You will do anything to create an environment where that person will somehow become fulfilling. You ignore all realities except your own intense emotional needs, never realizing that you are displacing control in a way that will never allow you to heal.

There are other similarities too. The love addict often establishes a relationship pattern that mimics the patterns set up by the drug addict. There will be a certain rhythm to her love affairs. It might involve marriage or living together; it might involve a dating pattern that includes set activities. Often there will be an expectation of hearing from the person by telephone a certain number of times per day or per week, and further expectations for the number of meals eaten together, movies seen, sports events enjoyed, and sexual encounters (intercourse, kissing, hugging, cuddling, etc.). There is intense discomfort if the frequency decreases, and rising expectations if the frequency increases.

In a healthy relationship, if the daily pattern is interrupted, such as when someone has to leave town to visit a sick relative or attend a business meeting, there is loneliness. The couple may talk by telephone or write each other love letters. They will look forward to the day they are again together to discuss what happened while they were apart. But the love addict does not experience normal loneliness. Instead, she feels pain, fear, and a sense of uneasy helplessness. Like a drug addict going through withdrawal, the love slave has an ache that is intensely personal. It can only be eased by the return to the old pattern, or one that is even more intense.

The healthy relationship causes the lovers to say, "I missed you" when the separation ends. The love slave experiences feelings, rarely verbalized at the time, that say, "I am hurting without you because I have to look inside and see an emptiness. I have a hole I'm using you to fill. I am not whole."

Class and Addiction

When Freud began his studies in nineteenth-century Europe, he found that social class determined addiction, with the wealthy elite the most likely to become love addicts. We are seeing the same thing today. Addictive tendencies are found in all racial, ethnic, and economic groups, of course. Studies show that low-income minority members frequently start with drugs like crack cocaine and heroin; low-income whites usually start with alcohol. Middle-income whites and minorities are likely to use cocaine, alcohol, or both. And high-income individuals, regardless of their ethnic background, are likely to start either with love addiction or a combination of love addiction and the drugs of choice of the middle-income group. But all of them are going through the same emotional turmoil.

Why is love addiction more prevalent among the upper-income group? Part of the answer simply has to do with what they can get away with. The men and women who hold high-status jobs and a position in the economic elite often avoid alcohol abuse because it is too easily spotted. Likewise, though they may enjoy illegal substances such as cocaine, they have learned that they must use it in moderation. This means that if they want to avoid the problems of their past without having to face the pain of healing, they must seek an alternate form of escape. For them, the answer is to seek a love object. They can afford to wine and dine the love object, even if they are married and have families. They can afford to rendezvous at motels and hotels. They can afford to add an extra person on a business trip, then hide the bills so their spouse does not learn the truth.

The addiction to another person, then, is just a different kind of self-destructive behavior for the very troubled man or woman who is a puppet of the past. And because we romanticize obsessive love, there is seldom friendly intervention, as with drug abuse; there is certainly no disgrace; and there is continual (and uninformed) forgiveness. The love that in a healthy individual is given to the ego, as Freud has shown, is moved to someone who can never provide the desired support. The love slave externalizes what can only be handled successfully within. For all these reasons, love addiction must be seen as every bit as serious, troubling, and in need of healing as an addiction to drugs, alcohol, and nicotine.

Chapter 6

The Recovery Program

There are two aspects to the recovery program you will read about in this book. The first is internal. In working the program, you will gain an understanding of how you were a puppet of your past, learning in the process how to live your life in full control as a healthy adult.

The second part of the program might be considered external. There is a natural depression that comes from being in a love-addicted relationship. Your life is not being lived in the manner you would like. You are seldom allowing yourself to experience a full range of emotions. And it is easy to slip into self-destructive habits that enhance your feelings of depression and hopelessness.

The two most common such habits are isolation and a poor diet. Many love addicts unconsciously avoid daylight. Some, for example, hold back from looking closely at their intimate relationships by avoiding them as much as possible. They go to work early and return home late. They stay in the office building or commute inside cars, buses, subways, or other conveyances. For whatever reason, they do not get out in the daylight on a regular and continuous basis. As a result, they do not manufacture that form of Vitamin D that acts as a natural tranquilizer.

Diet can also be a problem. The use of sugar, the inadequate intake of stress-fighting vitamins, and similar factors can make effective change quite difficult. As you are working the program that follows (and even after you have been healed of your love addiction), you may find that the lifestyle suggestions at the end of this book assure long-lasting happiness in ways you never thought possible.

Facing Up to the Fantasy
The first step toward ending your love addiction requires what is known as scanning or reviewing your past. Everyone has significant experiences in their formative years. Sometimes these influence

your career choice. Sometimes these affect your self-esteem. Sometimes these determine how you look at those of a different race, ethnic group, and/or religion. And a few of the significant experiences of your past affect how you relate to others in an intimate way.

Love addiction is not about life as it exists. Love addiction is about fantasy and myth. You may be perfectly suited for your love object, but as a love slave, you will not know this. Instead of seeing the person objectively as a whole person, you are in love with an idea, in love with love. You project characteristics onto the person with whom you are having a relationship. Then you relate to that individual as though the projection is truth, believing that the love relationship can fulfill your wants and perceived needs. Sometimes you are correct. Usually you are not. Yet you will not see the difference until you are healed.

You may be drawn to the individual's physical appearance, professional image, wealth, or some other characteristic that has little or nothing to do with the full person. The security of feeling yourself loved seems more important than anything else. A healthy relationship, on the other hand, involves mutual friendship, comfort, and passion. You are emotionally vulnerable to the other person just as he or she is vulnerable to you.

Love addicts are like members of an audience in a movie theater. They are sharing their existence with a two-dimensional person playing out a fantasy role on the screen of life. Unfortunately, this situation cannot be tolerated by the love object if he or she is involved in the relationship for non-neurotic reasons. And since most love addiction relationships include an emotionally healthy individual, they are doomed to the failure the love addict so greatly fears—unless the love slave overcomes his or her addiction.

Francesca's Story

Francesca discovered this reality after working the program in this book. Her parents had been brilliant intellectuals, living in New York's Greenwich Village during the era of Bohemian lifestyles, coffee shop debates about politics and the arts, and poetry readings. They were as intense in their play together as they were in their work, and both earned Ph.D. degrees—her father in philosophy, her mother in romance languages. Their lives were a mixture of passion and scholarship, and Francesca's birth came as a surprise to them.

Francesca was five years old when her mother died. She had

developed cancer, and by the time it was diagnosed, it was too late to help her. The cancer had spread through her lymphatic system, infecting several parts of her body. She languished a year between diagnosis and death, and her husband was emotionally overwrought. He tried to spend every moment he could with his wife, the couple's friends taking care of their daughter as much as possible. The university where he had obtained a job as an associate professor was generous with its help during the course of his wife's illness, but once she passed away, they expected him to return to a full course load.

Francesca's father seemed never fully to recover from his wife's death. He became distant and withdrawn from his daughter, meeting her physical needs but never emotionally committed to his growing child. He became a respected educator and author, was tenured at the university, and presented scholarly papers at international gatherings. His daughter was an afterthought.

Life was lonely for Francesca. She and her father had an apartment just off campus, and his students frequently acted as her sitter. She was comfortable in a world of what, to her, were adults. Yet she could never get her father's love.

Francesca tried everything she could think to do. She tried studying languages when they were offered in her school, then discovered that her interest was uncomfortable for her father. She increasingly looked like her mother, and the closer her interests to those of his late wife, the more her father seemed to withdraw to his study.

Francesca became involved with track and field in her high school. Although she did not deliberately sabotage her education as some children do when experiencing similar home lives, she did try to get approval in a way that was different from what she knew of her mother. She was a swimmer and competed against children in schools in the neighboring communities. Sometimes her father went to see her compete, and sometimes he did not. She was never certain until she saw him in the stands whether he would actually come, and when he did, she did her best to win. She was never a gifted athlete, but she worked hard, always seeking praise that did not come.

Once Francesca was in college, she began dating serious, scholarly males. She told her friends that she had no interest in the more aggressive males who approached her. She respected a man's mind. What she did not say, because she did not realize what she was doing, was that she was only going after males who were cold and distant. It was not the intellect of the men she was subconsciously seeking. Rather, it was the fact that they did *not* return her affection. She had to be the aggressor, making dates, suggesting activities they might do together, even seeking the first kiss.

Francesca tried to be whatever the men wanted. She changed her major to match the interest of her love of the moment so often that her faculty adviser warned her that either she settle down to one main course of studies or she would need an extra year or two to graduate. She tried dressing conservatively. She tried dressing like her idea of "a vamp." She worked late nights in the library because one of the males studied best at night. She arose early to take long walks at first light when another one of the men she was dating said that was what he liked to do. After college, when she was dating an assistant professor at the school they had both attended, she would stop by his apartment to clean, do his laundry, and cook meals that could be stored in the freezer compartment.

When Francesca first came to see me, it was obvious that she had woven a fantasy around her father's existence. In her mind, her parents had had the greatest love affair of all times. It was more intense than Antony and Cleopatra, Romeo and Juliet, or any of the other couples of history and literature. Her father had had his heart broken by her mother's death, and no woman had been good enough to break through the encrusted scar tissue of his heart in order to restore his love.

"I tried, Dr. Green," she told me. "I did everything I could. But I was only his daughter."

And he was a very selfish man, I thought to myself. Imagine a widower with a young child, the offspring of a supposedly beloved union, whom he ignored. The child was supposedly important to his wife, yet he refused to nurture and love Francesca as she needed, wanted, and had a right to expect. Loving Francesca was the same as loving his wife. Rejecting Francesca was a selfish act that belied the grief he supposedly felt. Perhaps her father simply loved the image of his wife, not the substance. Perhaps their marriage was in shambles at the time of her death, becoming healthy and strong only in the diminished hindsight of grief. Whatever the case, I ached for Francesca's inner child, the little girl still hurting, still causing her desperately to seek what she had too long been denied.

Francesca was playing out the role of loving seductress healing the broken-hearted object of her affection. Each man she chose was as cold and distant as her father had been. In her fantasy, each man also desperately wanted to be loved. He was holding in his emotions until the right woman came along and touched his heart. The moment the man responded with a hint of passion, he would be cured and they would live happily ever after.

Not surprisingly, it did not happen. She could take a man to bed, of course. She could make him grateful for her help. She could willingly be his doormat, his slave, his wildest fantasy if he but asked. Yet she could not change a man who was cold, self-centered, emotionally abusive, and a user, the very characteristics she came to see in her father.

The final emotional blow for Francesca came when one of the men she had been dating brought home another woman for sex. She was in his apartment, doing his laundry, and the girlfriend was shocked by her presence. "Francesca?" he laughed. "She's part pal and part maid. I can't have any pets here, so I have Francesca."

Then they both laughed and went into the bedroom, closing the door while she was still in the living room. The projected fantasy had become a harsh, intensely painful reality, and she knew she was out of control.

Dating Your Parents
You may be like Francesca, projecting a fantasy onto a real person, then forever being doomed to a failed relationship.

Or you may be like Herb, recognizing that you are miserable in your relationship most of the time. He told me that Naomi, his love object, was so beautiful that he was the envy of every man he knew. Heads turned whenever he walked through a restaurant with her on his arm. But there was constant tension in the relationship, a feeling of gloom except during those moments of intimacy when he felt it was all worth it. She was too special to lose, no matter what the cost of maintaining the relationship.

Love involves misery, Herb told me. Everyone knows that. "Look at all the novels, the movies, the popular song lyrics. Everyone suffers for love. I just happen to love someone more special than anyone else."

Naomi told Herb that he would not be happy with anyone else. No one could ever please him the way she did. No other woman would be right for him. "I know she's telling the truth," he explained. "I see how unhappy I am when we're apart, and I want to do anything I can to please her. That's my goal in life and I can't think of anything I'd rather be doing. If I can please her, then she'll please me and we'll have a wonderful life together."

There are many people like Herb. If your love addiction follows his pattern, then you are probably convinced that you are in the best possible relationship with the ideal person. You feel that you will never know greater happiness than you have found with the object of your affection. Your love object has brought you just enough pleasure with just enough frequency that you constantly live on hope.

Terry was constantly involved with men who specialized in back-handed compliments. Typical was her latest relationship with Isaac. She came to me all excited after attending a formal dinner party celebrating the fiftieth anniversary of the founding of the law firm where he worked. "I don't know why I've been so concerned about my relationships," Terry told me. "Isaac was so attentive last night. He even told me I looked beautiful in the evening gown that's going to set me back all my lunch money for the next zillion years."

Terry was so bubbly, her joy was infectious. Yet I suspected something was wrong. Isaac had been no different from the other men she had discussed in therapy, and all of them were what some people call "put-down artists." We talked about the evening in more detail, and the subtle underlayers of the destructiveness of the relationship began to emerge.

As it turned out, Isaac never said Terry looked beautiful. Instead he told her that "You don't look your usual frumpy self." Although he made comments about the breasts of every woman at the party, his only comment about Terry's attractive figure was, "at least I don't worry about your strapless dress falling down." He told Terry what to eat so she wouldn't spill anything on her clothes. He told her what to drink so she wouldn't embarrass him by getting drunk. And when he introduced her to friends who hadn't met her yet, he said, "This is Terry. She's one of the drudges at the bank." The fact that she had a Master's degree in business, was a certified public accountant, and was in line for top management was never mentioned. In fact, she was far more respected in her field than he was in his, and her future held greater potential.

"Normally he doesn't compliment me at all," Terry continued. "But last night . . . ."

It was business as usual. Destructive. Emotionally abusive. Obvious to anyone but Terry until she took the test in chapter 2 and began reviewing her childhood.

Terry's parents should have made a comfortable living. Her father worked for the Post Office as a letter carrier, and her mother was hostess at one of a chain of expensive restaurants. They lived in a small community where the cost of living was low, and Terry was what might have been called a "low-maintenance" only child. She didn't need unusual dental care. She didn't need glasses. And she had only the routine illnesses of childhood that all kids get. The problem was that her parents wanted to be wealthy, and they kept investing in get-rich-quick schemes that never quite panned out.

Most of the investments were in marketing schemes that were supposed to be similar to, though more profitable than, Avon, Mary Kay, Tupperware, and other legitimate programs. Her parents chose companies that required a high fee to join and another high fee for samples. Eventually it became obvious that the money was made through the selling of "franchises" and samples to gullible people like Terry's parents. They always took a loss, and they always seemed to fall further and further into needless debt in their pursuit of wealth.

Terry's parents were constantly frustrated. They also wondered aloud if they wouldn't have been better off without the expense of a child. "You're the one who got me drunk," her mother would yell at her father.

"So how was I to know the condom had a hole in it large enough for such an ugly little thing to slip through," he'd yell back. It was years before Terry fully understood her father's meaning, but even when she was confused by his words, she knew they were not loving.

Inevitably such banter led to laughter as her mother admitted that Terry was, indeed, quite homely. The truth was that Terry was not only a beautiful woman, she also looked exactly like her own mother, a fact her mother could not handle. Terry brought pictures of the two of them at the same stages of growing up, and they might have been twins. Yet Terry said, "See, Dr. Green, how beautiful Mother was and how ugly I was by comparison? No wonder she was ashamed of me."

Terry's self-hate made no sense, of course. But a child believes her parents, and Terry's parents managed to convince her that she left everything to be desired. When she got good grades in school, they told her that she must have "really bamboozled those teachers." When she got her first job, they told her she'd probably lose it in a week. "You're so irresponsible, you can't even keep your bedroom straightened up."

Eventually it seemed as though whenever Terry interacted with her parents, they made fun of her. She tried everything to please them, but there was no way. They were unhappy with their lives, and they found it easier to mock Terry than to admit to their own failings.

Ironically, had Terry's parents not been so greedy, they would have been fine. Together they earned far more than they spent on the necessities of life. Their savings alone would have amounted to a substantial estate by retirement. "I tried to show them that when I became an accountant," Terry said. "But they just told me I wasn't a striver. I didn't know what it was to pursue a dream. Hell, getting out of the house, getting an education, getting off on my own . . . . Those were dreams, realistic ones, and I achieved them. Their mockery couldn't change that."

Terry's problem was that she did not accept her past. She desperately wanted her parents' love and respect. She wanted them to see that she had made it, that they shouldn't think of themselves as failures because of their financial setbacks. They should look at what she had done and recognize that their success was in the way she turned out.

That never happened, of course. Dramatic reconciliations seldom occur in the manner we would like. Instead, Terry was drawn to a succession of destructive men she wanted to love her. If she could get them to treat her with respect, it would be the same as gaining parental love. Yet because their temperaments were so similar to that of her parents, her dream was never fulfilled. She remained obsessed with a fantasy that could never be achieved. She constantly, almost desperately, sought pleasure from men who would never provide her with more than the back-handed compliments Isaac had given her.

Once Terry worked the program, she began the acceptance of herself for who she was, not who her parents told her she had been. She realized that her parents had never truly known her. They had been so concerned with their own world that her life had been of secondary importance. They fed her, clothed her, and sheltered her. They sent her to school. They made certain she was never physically abused. Yet they never really talked with her. There was no sharing. There was no interest in her hopes and dreams. There wasn't even an effort to involve her with their work, though there were numerous minor chores she could have handled had they but asked. Such chores would have made her feel a part of the family, instead of feeling like someone's abandoned pet—reluctantly accepted, cared for, yet obviously never wanted.

"I'm dating my parents!" Terry exclaimed after working the program in this book. "I'm seeking men who are as lousy at being lovers and friends as my parents were at having a child. I couldn't wait to get out of the house when I was young. Why should I waste my time on losers like these idiots?"

And that was when Terry began to end her love addiction. No longer would she need to be like a beaten puppy desperately happy for even another dog's discarded bone.

I have sometimes asked an extreme love addict to remember the exact date and approximate time when he enjoyed intimacy so pleasurable that he will do anything to repeat it. Usually this means sexual intercourse, but there are those who talk of times when they were doing little more than taking a walk, truly communicating on an interpersonal level, each vulnerable to the other, each gaining pleasure from the other. They have experienced this so seldom that they do not realize it is the natural, spontaneous, and routine result of a healthy relationship. Often they have been convinced by the other person that it can only happen when he or she has been properly pleased, and they spend up to several hours a day in its pursuit. They will buy their love object presents, do those things the love object wants to do, regardless of their own interests. If this seems to reflect your own problems, then the approach that worked for Herb will also work for you.

The first step is to scan the period when similar problems have arisen. Perhaps the man or woman with whom you are miserable, yet to whom you are devoted, is your first serious relationship. More likely you are in the same circumstances as Terry and Herb. When Herb reviewed his past, he told me about his earlier relationships with Shirley, Linda, and Esther. Each was beautiful. Two were blondes, the third a brunette. They were tall, with excellent figures kept firm and shapely by regular exercise. They were intelligent, well-educated, and had good jobs, but it was their looks that mattered most. All of them fit the slang term in use at the time—"drop-dead gorgeous." He was proud to be with them. He was convinced that pleasing them so that they would have sex with him, go out with him, be seen with him, was what he must do with his life. He never shared their interests, or at least he never mentioned the things that gave him pleasure for fear that they would tell him they were incompatible. Instead he was like a puppy dog, walking by their sides but only in the directions in which they would lead.

Each of these past relationships had failed, causing him great pain. The women became tired of him. They felt that he had no life, no excitement. They wanted to know him better and claimed that he acted as though there was some invisible barrier between them and his true feelings. "Tell me what you want and I'll do it," he would say to them.

"Just be yourself," they would reply. "Let me know you."

"But what if you don't like the real me? What if you can't love that person?"

"I can't love what I don't know," they had ultimately protested, drifting into different relationships. Only Naomi had stayed with him so far, and she had her own emotional problems, delighting in seeing how he would respond each time she made new demands on him.

Terry had been the perfect verbal punching bag for a series of men. Secure in her job with the bank, knowledgeable, and in command of her daily activities, she always made herself compliant. She did not believe the words of other men who were interested in her when they told her she looked beautiful, that they admired the brilliance of one of her reports, or that she was the most capable manager they had ever encountered. She was embarrassed by compliments. More than being modest, she always felt undeserving. "It was easier for me to be told I was 'less of a piece of shit than when I was in high school,' as one of the guys I met at my tenth high school reunion said, than to take a heartfelt compliment. I didn't like feeling worthless; I just was comfortable with it. I had heard such things all my life. If someone said something nice, and if I realized they might be right, I panicked. It was like, 'Whoa, step back here. I don't know who they're talking about, but it can't be me!'"

If You're Miserable, It's Time to Change

As you look at your earlier relationships, I think that you will make discoveries similar to those of Francesca, Herb, and Terry. Each past relationship resulted in some degree of unhappiness you have never overcome. Each time you subjugated your own personality in order to ensure that you would please the person with whom you were involved. You were convinced that you could not find happiness with anyone else. You were convinced that you might lose that person at any instant and had to do whatever was necessary to avoid such a "catastrophe." Anything, that is, except be the "real you."

In Herb's case, he kept stressing how beautiful the women were. That was important to him, and it was the one aspect of the relationships that he stated over and over again. "They were each so beautiful . . ." he sighed. "And they all dumped me. They used me and dumped me, yet I tried so hard to please them. I just don't know what it all means. I just don't know what's going to happen to me."

Is this story a familiar one? Each relationship gave Herb a terrible quality of life. His fantasy had always been that he loved the women and they loved him. His reality was that he had always been miserable. The only happiness came from being with the women and giving them pleasure, whatever that meant, so that they might, in turn, please him somewhat.

For example, Herb told me that in August of 1989, Naomi told him he was a good lover. It was the only compliment she had ever paid him, and she had not repeated it. "But she said it that once and I know I can get her to say it again if I just work hard enough." He also never forgot the date the statement was made.

Herb was experiencing a projection onto his love object. He had placed a fantasy relationship on a real person's body and was fighting desperately to nurture that fantasy.

Terry convinced herself that anything any man in her life did was always more exciting than her work and personal interests. One of her lovers liked to go to sports bars, order a pitcher of beer, and sit watching a baseball game.

"I had nothing against baseball—I just found it boring. Played correctly, nothing happens. The pitcher throws the ball to the catcher, and the batter swings at air. The lower the score by which a team wins, the better the players.

"It isn't so bad in a ballpark. There you can watch the crowds, who always put on a good show. You can buy hot dogs and peanuts and ice cream that make you sick to your stomach by the time the game reaches the eighth inning. It's like being part of a show, and I don't mind that. But watching it on television just reminds me of how boring it is. And watching it in a sports bar means a lot of heavy drinkers are going to be sitting around making nasty remarks, something they probably would not have been doing if they were sober.

"But I went to those damned sports bars week after week. We'd watch games coming live by satellite. We'd watch games being fed by cable because of blackout rules near the stadium. We'd watch reruns of games on the nights when no one was playing. And when I suggested we at least go to the stadium, he was stunned. He couldn't imagine having to sit through something like that. Then he was hurt because he thought I might not love the places like he did. Naturally I lied."

Terry also took up water skiing, which she hated, and rock climbing, and she was considering bungee jumping—a sport that terrified her but delighted the "Mr. Wonderful" of the moment. "When I realized that I was willing to think about leaping off some crane somewhere and bouncing around on rubber bands, I figured I needed to have my head examined!"

Terry and Herb were both convinced that even the least desirable of their love interests was somehow special, certainly better than they were. A common trait of love slaves is to keep their love objects on a pedestal. The person can do little wrong. The person needs no help, no support in what he or she does. The person is viewed as all-good, all-nurturing, competent, and resourceful.

When there is a problem in the mind of the love slave, the cause is external. For example, the love slave may say, "He's a really great artist, but none of the advertising agencies will give him a chance." She refuses to look at the fact that he lacks the training in the kind of equipment and design needed in the profession. Or the love slave may say, "She's such a great cook, and she'd so love to be in the business of catering, I don't know why none of the companies will snatch her up." Yet he knows full well that each time she applies for such a job, she is told where and how to gain the experience necessary to do the kind of mass preparation on which the caterer's business depends. And each time she is accepted for such training, she refuses to take the courses, claiming she already knows enough "if they really wanted me."

Friends of the love slave see how unrealistic the person is being. There are no blinders on their eyes. But the love slave has such a low sense of self-esteem, he or she projects only positive traits on the person with whom he or she is having a relationship.

At the same time, the love slave is often intensely jealous. This is because of the insecurity of the person with low self-esteem.

It is natural for each of us to be drawn to many men or women, not just the person to whom we have made a commitment. Physical appearance, body chemistry, and numerous other superficial factors make others attractive, giving us a sense of pleasure when we look at them from across a room or office. Healthy, mature individuals are regularly inclined to look at whomever they find beautiful or handsome. The emotionally healthy individual knows all this, and he is not jealous when his wife or lover looks at another man. She is not jealous when her husband or lover looks at another woman. And this carries over to those couples who have a same-sex orientation. But the love addict is always jealous. Sometimes the jealousy is internalized, the love slave saying, "Look at the way she looks at that person over there. I know I won't keep her much longer. Already she is straying. Maybe she has already had an affair. Maybe it's just a matter of time. But why would anyone want to stay with me? I don't have anything to offer. I'm not attractive. I'm not rich. I'm not exciting. Already she is setting up the next affair."

At other times it is externalized. There are jealous rages, and the love object may be naive enough to think that they are flattering. But the idea of two boys or two girls fighting over a person is immature at best, demeaning at worst. In the extreme, it is either the act of a couple of kids on the school grounds trying to impress the girl or boy of their dreams, or it is a sense of the loved one as a possession. "My man" or "my woman" seems to be the attitude, and the fight is to assure continued possession. In fact, the only thing that separates such an experience from an animal encounter where wild creatures lock horns and fight, is that humans cannot own each other. We can, however, enslave each other. We can kidnap and hold each other in physical and psychological restraints. We can kill our rivals, then seduce the beloved, or use violence to capture through intimidation. But we cannot force love. Emotional commitment cannot be forced; neither can psychological monogamy.

Constant jealousy is inappropriate behavior for an adult. And great jealousy is almost always a clue that the person is a love slave being destroyed by the fantasy life of the unconsciously obsessed lover. This fantasy life, which results in rages, also leads to a misreading of the love object, to the putting of that person on a pedestal.

There are times the love object is competent and successful in the way the love slave believes. But because the person is but a screen on which a fantasy is projected, when the love object is in crisis, the love slave often appears callous. The unexpected death of a loved one, the loss of a job, or some other personal crisis is normally a time for lovers to grow closer together. The person who is frightened, depressed, or otherwise in need of emotional support expects the lover to help. Yet frequently, either that help isn't there or the love slave becomes demanding.

"You know I'm no good with funerals. Everyone's all emotional and I never know the right thing to say, the way you do. Why don't I drop you off and meet you afterward?"

Or "You're feeling bad? How do you think I feel? What am I going to do with you moping around all day about being out of work? If you can't keep a job with all your skills, what do you think is going to happen to me?"

Or, "I wish you could be like you were. Your depression is making my life miserable. I wish you'd cheer me up like you used to do."

It is for these reasons and more that spouses and lovers who have been placed on a pedestal almost always resent such worshipful adoration. I have had many complain to me, "He doesn't really know who I am. I've lived with this person for ten years and he still doesn't know me. I love him, but I can't go on like this. The relationship is too one-sided, and I'm the only one who's noticed." If you are a love slave, the key to recognizing the need for change in this circumstance is the fact that your arrangement, like Herb's and Terry's, has only resulted in emotional pain and misery. The quality of your life is miserable, and it is this quality that we are going to change.

It is said that the child is parent to the adult. This means that the learned behaviors of childhood are reflected in our actions as adults. The examples of our parents, how they live, how they react to each other, and what they say to us, have great meaning as we grow. They are our role models for adult behavior. We may hate what they do and how they treat us, but those actions become a part of our subconscious programming, to be imitated when we are establishing our own adult relationships. This is true even when we knew as children that they were wrong, even when we vowed to be different when we grew up.

We seek the food our parents prepared for us because the taste is comforting. We discipline our children based on the ways we were disciplined, even if we felt, at the time, that they were wrong. This is only one of the more obvious proofs of the influences we have experienced. If, when we were a child, our misdeeds were met with a beating involving our father's belt, when our own child misbehaves we are likely to grab the nearest belt to administer a spanking. This is not because the punishment is the best alternative. It is not because it is appropriate. It is because we are angry, the child needs to be punished, and the first thought we have is to punish in a manner that we associate with parent/child discipline from our own childhood.

This is true with the healthy childhood, not just the dysfunctional one. The idea of giving a child "time out" where he or she is relegated to a bedroom for a few minutes until tempers calm may be one that was learned when growing up. The same is true with talking to a child instead of thinking of striking first. But the love addict is reeling from negative influences, not positive ones.

A child who has not been given a strong sense of self-worth becomes an adult who will not feel confident about his or her abilities. A child who is desperately looking for parental love will, as an adult, transfer that search to the person he or she seeks for a relationship. But because they project fantasy into the marriage or affair, they end up having an intimate stranger, not by the other person's choice but their own. Fortunately, this subconscious programming can be changed. The first step is recognizing that it exists, and that only through understanding how we have been affected can we overcome our problems. Conscious awareness of the past is the start of healing.

Chapter 7

Taking a Fresh Look at Your Past

Each of us has childhood experiences that have shaped our present lives. Sometimes these were the result of one of our parents giving us destructive information. Sometimes these were the result of our misunderstanding the circumstances in which we were raised. Terry, for example, had parents who looked upon her as a nuisance in their endless drive for greater financial success. They blamed her for their failures, and not knowing any better, she accepted the blame. Yet when she reviewed the incidents from the viewpoint of each parent, she saw matters quite differently.

Terry's mother felt herself inadequate in life. She had not done particularly well in school. Her own father, Terry's grandfather, abandoned his wife when Terry's mother was in third grade. They lived in a small town, and Terry's grandmother was an object of either pity or scorn. Single parents were not common, and most married women feared Terry's grandmother would be on the make for their husbands. Others laughed at her behind her back, saying that she must be awfully frigid for a man to have left her. Terry's mother found herself ostracized from many of the school activities she wanted to join. She had friends, but they were loners, the girls who were excluded from the various "in" groups at school. She was told by her teachers and even the minister at her church that she would never amount to anything because she carried the stigma of her parents' divorce.

"She couldn't love me, Dr. Green," Terry realized. "She couldn't love herself. When I think about it, she was always putting herself down. If my father or I didn't like what she fixed for dinner, she'd agree that it was not very good. 'What do you expect from someone who comes from a family of losers,' she'd say. If one of their businesses went bad, she would say it was her fault.

"I don't think my mother even loved my father. He was just the one person who didn't belittle her for her parents' problems.

He had been a loner and an outcast himself, his parents dying when he was young. He had worked since he was fourteen, and though he was always reading something, he didn't think he was very intelligent. He seemed as amazed that my mother wanted him as she was by his interest. But instead of growing together, it was like they reveled in staying in quicksand together, even when there were plenty of opportunities to pull themselves out.

"They had no business having children. They couldn't really take care of themselves. Neither got to know me, and I think that whenever I was successful at something, it was like a slap in the face to them. It was a further reminder of how little they had achieved.

"There was nothing wrong with me, Dr. Green. The problem was with them. Yet I've been trying to live like the impression I had as a child was the right one, that I'll never be worth loving."

An emotionally abused child is constantly trying to determine what he or she did wrong. The child cannot understand that there is a difference between appropriate discipline and abuse. The child needs the parents' love and attention so completely that he or she will change rather than try to analyze what is taking place. This is why children blame themselves for the divorce of their parents. This is why children who lose a parent for any reason often try to modify their behavior in order to somehow effect the return of that parent, even if the parent has died.

Learning from Our Fathers

Herb, like Terry, eventually came to see his difficulties as a reflection of childhood needs. His problems included the feeling that he had to be with a beautiful woman. His wife was to be his queen, someone who would be worshiped and adored.

Herb also believed that loving someone else was all-encompassing. He believed that so long as he loved his wife, he would be happy. Yet he also "knew" that only a physically beautiful woman could be loved like that. And his own self-image was dependent upon the person he was with, not himself.

Knowing these facts about himself, Herb was asked to think about the times when he had heard these statements from one or both of his parents while a child. I had him start by looking at how his father thought about love and marriage. I wanted him to review his childhood teachings from his father's viewpoint, the same approach you should use when starting this exercise.

The first thought Herb had was that his mother was a beautiful woman when young. He remembered photographs of his mother taken when he was a small boy. She was strikingly beautiful, and his father was always proud to take her out, to show her off in front of other men. "'You're nothing without a beautiful woman,' my father always told me," Herb began to remember. "He said that a man should be a king. But a king cannot exist without a queen. It is the woman who makes the man special, so she had better be special herself. Looks. Beauty. Glamour. Style. That's what matters in life. It's all image if you want to be happy, and it takes a gorgeous woman to give you the right image. That's what he always told me and I know he was right. All the women I've been serious about have been beautiful. You've seen Naomi. Isn't she lovely?"

"Yes," I told him. "But there's far more to her than just her face and figure."

"It's the looks that matter. That's what my father always said and that's why he married my mother."

"Let's stop right there," I said to Herb. It is important to explore each discovery as it is made—a technique you should be doing with your own review of your childhood. Herb realized that his father taught him that his worth was based on the appearance of the woman on his arm. The real question now was how valuable a model this may actually have been in Herb's life. "Your father married a beautiful woman because that made him feel himself to be a king among men. Is that right?"

"Yes," Herb replied.

"Was your father happy with his life?"

"My father was a very unhappy man. He must have been happy earlier, of course. My parents had me, so he must have enjoyed the love of a beautiful woman at least once." He laughed at his little joke, then grew serious. "But he was always miserable, always trying to please my mother, always trying to get her to experiment with make-up and clothing. I remember that when she was in her late forties, he worked hard to be able to send her to a plastic surgeon in order to get her face lifted. Yet they seemed to drift apart, even though they stayed together. There was always tension between them, and he was always unhappy."

"As you are unhappy with Naomi?" I asked.

"Yes, but life is like that. If you truly love someone, you suffer for that love."

"Yet you can only love a beautiful woman? Tell me, Herb, have you ever liked a woman just for herself? Have you ever met a woman who made you happy just as a friend?"

Herb paused a moment, thinking. Then he smiled, the first expression of pleasure I had seen on his face since he came to see me. "There was one. Barbara. She was a law clerk in the first office where I worked.

"It was rather odd," he continued. "There was nothing special about her. She was short, an adequate figure though a little overweight from sitting around and eating too much junk food in college. But what a mind. She seemed to know everything about everything. She was in love with learning, yet she could apply what she learned. We'd go out for coffee and a sandwich at a deli when we both had to work late, start talking, then discover three or four hours had passed." He laughed and said, "I remember one time the two of us had to work all night because we had a project that had to be done by morning and we spent four hours just talking in this coffee shop near the office. We didn't realize how much time had gone by until the owner threw us out so he could lock the doors. We took turns working and catnapping until the project was complete. We would have been done early if we hadn't gotten so caught up with each other over what should have been a short dinner break."

"Did you date her?"

"No. I was going with Ann at the time. She was a model and really stunning. She said she thought that having sex with a lawyer was the greatest thing in the world, except maybe for having sex with a doctor. She eventually married a surgeon, but when I was with her, I felt on top of the world." His face seemed sad as he talked about her, no longer animated as it had been when he was discussing Barbara.

"And then you dated Barbara?"

"No. Then came Marilyn. I told you, Barbara just wasn't physically attractive."

"Yet she made you happy. You liked Barbara. You spent time with Barbara. As we were talking about her, your face seemed to light up from the memory."

"I guess I was happy with her." He seemed surprised by the admission.

"You know," I told Herb. "The purpose of life is not to be miserable. We are happiest when we select our mates because we enjoy being with them. Not on so superficial a level as whether or not they are physically beautiful. On a deeper level, dealing with the whole person."

"But my father . . ."

"Your father was wrong. He was a miserable man with his queen on his arm. And what happened when your mother began to lose her beauty through the natural aging process? Unless she died young, she must have been unhappy as well. Even face lifts can't turn back the clock for very long."

"She didn't die young. She lived into her seventies, and he seemed to get more miserable and depressed with each passing year. He spent most of his time going to bars or hanging out at the American Legion Post he belonged to. It was like he didn't want to be seen with her, because she had become an embarrassment to him when she lost her looks."

"Is that what will happen with you and Naomi?"

"I don't know. I hadn't thought that far ahead. Naomi's the most beautiful woman I've ever known. I'm certain she'll be beautiful when she's older."

"But what if she isn't? You're already unhappy while she is beautiful. What do you think will happen to your relationship later on?"

Herb wasn't quite ready to look at that issue, so we continued looking at his childhood. He told me about his older brother, who used to have beautiful girls calling him all the time when he was a teenager. By the time he was in college, he had his choice of any woman he wanted on campus, and he played the field, much to his parents' delight. They were quite proud of their older son's popularity. They bragged about him to friends in front of Herb, reinforcing Herb's belief that he could only know happiness by the side of a beautiful woman.

Next Herb talked about the popular music he listened to all the time. The music was usually love songs that talked about how, with love, everything was perfect. All you needed was love to ensure happiness. Nothing else mattered.

He mentioned movies and advertisements as well. Always there were images of beautiful women on the arms of the men who were obviously the best-looking, most successful, and happiest individuals in the room. Anything could be yours with a beautiful woman by your side. Looks were what counted.

"Yet it was this Barbara, a woman you said lacked the great physical beauty of women like Naomi, who brought you happiness. Could it be that your father's way was wrong?"

Herb was horrified by what I was suggesting. He felt guilty criticizing his father, a reaction you are likely to find in yourself as you scan your relationship with your own parents. Again I asked him to look at his childhood, this time exploring what he felt himself to be in his father's eyes.

This time Herb realized that his father had always seen him as the extension of his mother. She was the perfect queen. He was the perfect prince.

But Herb wasn't perfect. He was a normal little boy. He got dirty. He didn't always get the highest grades of which he was capable when in school. He forgot to do his chores or deliberately avoided work that was his responsibility to get done. He was lazy at times, irresponsible, and just like every other child developing into adulthood. Unfortunately, a normal child was not what his father demanded to fulfill his fantasy. He needed perfection from his son just as he needed it from his wife. But while a certain amount of projected fantasy colored his thoughts about his wife, there was no such projection onto his son. He made the boy feel himself to be a continuing disappointment, a failure.

Herb's self-esteem was shattered. He could do nothing right. He was desperate to please his father, yet he could not. He had to be perfect and constantly berated himself for falling short of that goal.

In your own life, if your past is like Herb's, you will typically fall into one of two categories. One is the desire to be a perfectionist. You are uncomfortable with anything you do unless you feel certain that it is 100-percent accurate. You are never able to take pleasure in your accomplishments because they are never without some minor flaw that proves you have fallen short of where you were taught you should be.

At the other extreme is psychologically giving up. You "know" you can do nothing right so you don't even want to try. Why pursue victory if failure is inevitable?

There are obviously all kinds of behavior patterns in between these two ends, but they will all lean toward one direction or the other. Interestingly, this is very much the same situation that occurs in a family where one or both parents are alcoholic. And like the adult child of an alcoholic, your relationship may be colored by how you react. The perfectionist may choose any love object because he or she takes responsibility for the relationship. Any failing is the result of the love addict's not being good enough or working hard enough.

By contrast, the person who has essentially given up, accepting him or herself as a failure, may become involved with a destructive narcissist. Consciously the love addict with low self-esteem still feels that he or she has control of the ultimate success of the relationship. Subconsciously he takes perverse pleasure in the constant rejection, knowing it is futile to try to please the love object, yet feeding on the other person's destructiveness. The relationship becomes emotionally and, at times, physically sado-masochistic, with the love addict on the receiving end of the abuse. Herb was fortunate, though, because despite his self-hate, his latest love object was an inherently good woman.

Admittedly I am condensing the work we did. You will need a few hours, days, or weeks, depending upon how quickly you become comfortable with your past, in order to sort through your childhood as it relates to your father. Some people are able to handle the task in one sitting. Others must gradually assimilate what they are learning. In all cases you will find that the effort brings results quicker than you expect because you only need to review those areas that have stimulated your present thinking about relationships, not your entire life. What is important is that you keep reviewing what you were taught by your father until you understand what happened and where you learned what you now see is inappropriate behavior.

Many of the men and women who come to my office to be guided through the program set aside time each day to meditate and work the exercises. They scan incidents they have reviewed in the past as well as incidents that are just now coming to conscious memory. They repeat what they have done, what you are being taught in this book, until they have understanding and self-acceptance. Invariably they are successful, and invariably their lives are enriched by the experience.

Learning from Our Mothers

If your problem is similar to Herb's, the key issue is the question of quality of life. You are unhappy or you would not be working this program. Recognizing that your father was unhappy when he taught you to behave in the same manner that he did is an important step. You are repeating his discomfort, his poor quality of life, taking misery into a new generation. And all because you have focused on superficial characteristics instead of the whole person.

Now scan your childhood from your mother's perspective. Look at the messages she gave you, as well as her relationship with your father.

This time Herb saw two different messages. The first was the reinforcement of his dating beautiful women, not because of what she said to him but because of the way she showed her love to his older brother when all the girls were calling him. His mother was pleased with his brother's popularity, and Herb wanted to enjoy her approval as well.

But the second message surprised him. He realized that his mother was an unhappy, highly frustrated woman. She resented his father's attitude toward her. She felt her husband did not know her, that they had lived together for many years and raised two sons to manhood, yet all he saw was her physical appearance. He knew nothing about the qualities that made her unique, did not even know whether he might prefer her company to the men in the bars. She had dreamed about a companion in her old age. Instead she had only a bitter man who seemed to grow smaller in stature as she lost the radiant beauty in which he had taken such pride. She was angry with him for making her a fantasy instead of a friend.

"Is that what I've been doing?" Herb wondered aloud. At this time I took him through the next stage. I had him scan each failed relationship in his own life from the viewpoint of the beautiful women he had loved, each of whom had left him over the years. I had him start with his first serious relationship and then continue through to his present situation with Naomi.

Each time Herb looked at a relationship from the viewpoint of the woman, he saw that everything started perfectly. Both of them were happy being together. The woman seemed genuinely to enjoy his company. Yet after a few weeks or months, she began to resent him. She felt that he was not trying to grow in the relationship, that she was always a projection of his fantasies, that he was miserable when her real personality seemed to intrude on his mental creation.

Herb came to see that the destruction of his relationships was always his own doing. He placed the women on a pedestal and then projected on them qualities that they could never live up to. He would not let himself know and love the woman for herself. He had to make her into something she was not, causing great frustration and planting the seeds of destruction.

"But how can I be happy?" asked Herb. "Now you've shown me that I've destroyed every relationship I've ever had. That just proves I'm no good."

"Quite the contrary. First off, though that dark side of you, the side controlled by the incorrect teachings of your past, has led to problems, you have had relationships. Women have been drawn to you for yourself, turning away only when you insisted upon refusing to know them for who and what they were as individuals.

"More important, you have also known great happiness. You told me about Barbara, a woman you so enjoyed that time passed without your noticing. And she probably isn't the only such woman you have encountered. For all you know, Naomi could give you as much pleasure if you would stop trying to turn her into something she isn't."

Herb had to think about what his life had been. He could see that he was repeating his father's actions, and that his father had never been happy with his mother. It was his job to break the destructive pattern in his family, to ignore a woman's physical appearance and look deeper into the relationship.

Without help, the love addict often refuses to see the character flaw in a parent. This leads to the constant search for a "cure" to relationship problems that cannot be treated.

Charlene, for example, was the daughter of one of the most theatrical women one could ever expect to meet. The mother was a cosmetics salesperson for a large department store by day, but by night she was an actress I'll call Helena.

Helena adopted a single name for the stage in the way of Cher and Madonna. She was a barely adequate singer, a weak dancer, and the kind of actress who forms the stereotypical image of the worst of amateur theater. She appeared in numerous shows in small towns where a group of well-meaning people would rent the high school auditorium and put on two or three plays a year. Often the work was familiar—*Guys And Dolls*, *My Fair Lady*, *Harvey*, and the like. There were never enough competent people to fill the roles, so men and women like Helena were invariably cast. She would overact, of course, playing prima dona and being relegated to the back of the chorus as much as possible. Too much make-up was used to hide what she felt were the ravages of advancing age. Flamboyant clothing exaggerated what she called her "two best parts." And she lived for the days when publicity photos were taken for ads in the local newspapers. To serious performers, she was a clown, someone to laugh about behind her back.

Sometimes Helena tried out for professional shows and roles in television and radio commercials. She would go to open auditions—"cattle calls" as they are derisively known in the industry—and never get a part. She seldom read more than a sentence before she was thanked for coming with a "Don't call us, we'll call you." Yet Helena never realized she was making a fool of herself. She was waiting to be discovered at twenty, at thirty, at forty, and at fifty. She is now in her sixties and still believes that the next audition will be her big break.

Helena constantly talked of being "considered for a role opposite Al Pacino" or whichever other star was involved in the movie where she auditioned to be a face in the crowd. And she insisted that her daughter, Charlene, call her by her stage name. "They'll think we're best friends, not mother and daughter. God, it would be the kiss of death if anyone thought you were my brat," Helena used to laugh.

Helena was in love with herself. Her world was filled with self-delusional fantasy. She wanted attention. She wanted to be a star. And she wanted adulation, even from her family.

"I tried to please my mother," said Charlene. "At first I got involved with little theater work as a kid, thinking that would please her. Then, if I got a good role, she turned on me. When I was nine years old I was cast as Peter Pan in an abridged version of the kids' story. I don't think anyone in the play was older than eleven, and none of us were any good. We were part of a kids' drama class held every Saturday at the same theater where my mother did much of her work. Once a year they did some big production so that the parents would get all teary-eyed and pay anything the place charged for lessons. None of us ever went further than maybe doing something in a high school production, and I think most of us were there to please our mothers or fathers.

"Anyway, Helena was irate with me. She criticized my rehearsing. She criticized the way I did the role on stage. And when the audience gave us a standing ovation, something they gave to every kids' production, she was livid. 'You weren't that good, Charlene,' she told me. 'Audiences today have definitely lowered their standards, at least where you young people are concerned.' It was both bitchy and stupid.

"I got the message, though," Charlene continued. "I stopped trying to be in any more plays. I worked on scenery and helped the costumer. But I could see she didn't approve of my doing something in what she considered her exclusive domain."

There were numerous other hurts. Helena never was active in her daughter's school or personal activities. Some producer might call. Some director might call her back for a second reading.

Eventually Charlene's father left her mother and married a young waitress at a coffee shop near his office. "Helena said that he needed someone young to make him feel good," said Charlene. "I don't think it was that. I don't think either noticed the age of the other. His new wife was friendly, caring, genuinely interested in others. I think he found the contrast refreshing, though Helena would never think of herself as self-centered. She was 'career oriented.' She just never had a career, except in her own imagination."

Charlene's life was empty though she was well-cared-for, living in a small apartment that was modestly furnished, yet always with an eye for when "the photographers might drop by."

"I was a set prop. That was all. I needed nice dresses because they were what the daughter of Helena would wear at home. And when I wanted a pet, she told me I could have the same type of dog as some Broadway actress she admired. She actually cut the picture of the woman with her dog from the Sunday *New York Times* and took me to the ASPCA shelter to look for a match. I loved that dog, but I lived in constant fear that she would decide it had gone out of style and make me get rid of it."

Charlene did everything she could to make her mother proud of her, to gain her love. However, her mother's only true love was her reflection in the mirror. She was a monogamous narcissist. There was no room in her life for any other love, including her own daughter.

Charlene made this discovery only when she worked the program. "I just thought I was worthless growing up," said Charlene. "I hated my father for leaving us for another woman. How could he rebuke my mother's love, I wondered. And then I realized that maybe his leaving was also my fault. Since Helena was perfect, then I must be flawed."

Naturally, Charlene acted in the manner of so many love addicts. She was instinctively drawn to self-centered men. Each had the facade of strength, independence, and self-assuredness. And each was actually isolated within himself, a caricature of a lover.

For example, there was Tom, who, though professing undying love, tended to walk three or four paces ahead of Charlene as though he wasn't really with her. "He seemed to be advertising the fact that he stood alone, that I was not important in his life," she said.

Jeff insisted that she admire how he looked in the custom-tailored clothing he favored. He also wanted her to remember how he dressed from date to date so she could make comparisons. When they went to restaurants, she noticed that, all else being equal, the server would receive more money if Jeff was complimented than if the server said something nice to her.

Lawrence would study Charlene before they went out. Then he would have her sit in either the front passenger seat of his car or in the back, depending on how he felt she looked. He did not want to have someone who might detract from his image on the street.

"Each time I started a new relationship with a man, I felt certain I could make him love me. I would do anything for each of them. Anything. I was just lucky that they were too in love with themselves to care about sex. I would have become promiscuous, letting each do with me what he wanted in order to please him. As it was, we invariably broke up before going to bed, which was rather fortunate. Even beyond the moral issues involved for me, I had the feeling that the only way any of them would have been aroused would have been if they placed a photograph of themselves over my face."

Charlene had never been able to please her narcissistic mother, and as an adult her dating pattern was meant to correct that problem. She chose only self-centered men, then tried to gain a sense of self-worth through their love. Of course, they were never capable of loving anything but their reflections in the mirror. She was always frustrated, always hurt, always trying too hard for an impossible relationship.

Maxine was another patient of mine. Her problem came with angry parents she could never please. All her men were easily upset, yet because they were never physically violent towards her, she lied about them to herself. "They're impassioned. They're dedicated. They know who they are, what they believe, and are going after it." But after working the program she realized that they were carrying on for the sake of hearing themselves rail against something, anything, even if they knew nothing about it. They had no depth. They also never really did anything, much like her parents, who were forever fighting over something. But Maxine had never been able to bring peace to her family as a child, and since she saw that role as her job, she tried to bring peace to the angry men she dated.

Change: Hard, but Worth It

It is important to note that, even with the new understanding you gain from looking at your past from the viewpoint of each of your parents, you will not necessarily feel comfortable changing right away. Love addicts tend to generalize, just as they tend to fantasize. They often believe all men or all women to be like the ones to whom they are drawn. If they see that others are different, they find fault with them, a reason why they are not attracted to those who don't fit the image.

"All men are late for dates." "All women flirt." "All men get slovenly." "All women are obsessed with their make-up." "All men want is a pair of big breasts. They don't care about a woman's intellect or personality." "All women want a father figure. Sometimes dating feels more like incest the way they treat me." Such comments are used to reassure ourselves. If we lie to ourselves by saying that everyone with whom we might be involved is the same, why change our relationship? It "can't" get better and it might get worse.

This is not true, of course, as any former love addict can tell you. But the belief, and the fear that the fantasy is reality, often keep an individual from risking change.

New dating patterns are frightening. The growth of the AIDS problem has made many people delay physical intimacy more than in the past. When they are intimate, they usually take precautions for safer sex, and may go so far as to take blood tests first.

But there are other fears too, fears that are less likely to be spoken. "What if I drop Norman only to discover that Ben is no different? At least I always knew what to expect with Norman. Now I have to learn a whole different behavior pattern."

Or "What if my father/mother was right about me? At least Candace is foolish enough to accept me as I am. Someone else might not. I'd better not end the relationship, even though she keeps hurting me with her actions."

There are numerous ways in which we express our fears, yet they all stem from the same problem. We have survived in life with one pattern of behavior. It is known, familiar, and comfortable in the sense that it is predictable. Why should we change for something an outsider says is better when we're really not certain it will be?

It is impossible to argue with such a position, except to say that I have seen the changes in my friends and patients who were love addicts. I have seen men and women go from misery to self-acceptance to happiness. There were periods of loneliness. There were moments when it was necessary to fight the desire to return to the same kind of person who was "dumped" in the past. But the end result was always worth it. That's what they tell me. That's what those who have worked the program will tell you.

If you are a love slave, your life has been filled with false hope and emotional turmoil. You are living for a fantasy, for a "next time" that you instinctively know will never come. You are hurting enough to seek the help available through this book.

As a love addict, you are reacting to your partner in a manner that is not emotionally fulfilling. You are subverting your own needs and hopes for someone else. And nothing is working for you the way you expected.

Your relationships cannot make you any unhappier than you are now. If I am wrong, and given my experience with thousands of men and women like yourself over the years, I doubt that I am, you can always go back to your old ways. But for now, use your new recognition about yourself and your love life to facilitate change—beginning with the next step in healing, developing a positive self-image.

Chapter 8

Developing a Positive Self-Image

Uncovering the problems from your past is the first step towards healing. But it is only the first step! Developing a positive self-image is a crucial part of finding new happiness. Too many people forget this. They try to use their new knowledge as a way of perpetuating their sense of self-hate. "Of course," they may say. "I'm repeating patterns from my childhood. I've been such a fool! But, of course, I would be. Haven't I been stupid about things all my life? This just proves what I've always known. I don't know why anyone has anything to do with me."

Perpetuating a negative self-image is one of the easiest things any of us can do. Just being human assures that we are going to make daily mistakes. It is the nature of our existence. All life involves growth. We must challenge ourselves physically, emotionally, and intellectually or we will stagnate at best, decline at worst. Each time we go beyond the familiar, we are certain to fail, at least on occasion. The emotionally healed individual accepts this. The love addict may not, at least not during this early stage.

We have to remember that making mistakes is normal. Losing your keys, dropping a carton of eggs, running a stop sign—these are normal. And perpetuating the self-image created by your parents' reactions to you as a child is normal. There are love addicts who seek help at twenty-one, heal, and lead intensely happy lives for the next half-century or longer. There are others who do not come to me until they are in their fifties, their sixties, or even older. They, too, wish to heal, to change the pattern in which they have been living. And this is normal as well.

One woman in her late seventies explained to me that she realized she had a problem when she felt guilty throwing her boyfriend out of the trailer home they shared. She had a greater need for sex than he had desire, and she didn't want to die feeling unfulfilled. She had spent her entire life trying to please men, and now she wanted to please herself.

The woman's story was like the majority of stories told by love slaves, except that she felt guilty even considering talking about such matters. She was raised at a time when family secrets were not discussed publicly. You respected your parents by never considering their failings, much less mentioning them to a therapist. She knew she had been paying too great a price for too many years, and finally she decided to stop.

The circumstances that drove her to the decision seemed a bit humorous to me, but her pain was intensely real. And the program helped her heal. As she said, "You are never too old to want to feel better about yourself and your life."

Until you become uneasy about the pattern in your relationship(s), you are not likely to explore the reasons behind that pattern. Only then can you learn why that pattern developed, why it is now wrong for you, and how to break it—to shatter the subconscious psychological bondage of the love slave.

So instead of berating yourself for having been caught up in love addiction, you should congratulate yourself for taking this positive step. It does not matter when in our lives we change for the better. What matters is that we do change, and you should give yourself credit for courage.

Once you have uncovered the problems from your past, you need to reexamine yourself. You have been carrying low self-esteem as a part of your emotional make-up for the past several years. You have developed relationships based on self-hate. You have refused to look objectively at yourself.

Sit down with a pencil and paper and make a list of all your good characteristics. This is a time for objectivity, not modesty. I am not asking you to become a narcissist. If you are a religious person, you might begin by noting that you are a creation of God, a part of the life of this planet where everything has a purpose, whether we understand it or not. If you are not religious, your first entry might be the fact that you have had relationships. Members of the opposite sex have found you to be attractive enough to want to spend some time with you.

Be as thorough as possible. Are you working? Then obviously you earned the respect of the person who hired you.

Self-employed? Then you have shown courage and tenacity while trying to build your business.

Job hopping? Then you leave the kind of positive impression that causes employers to take a chance on you, despite a job history of not spending very long in any one position. And that job hopping also means that you can handle diversity, that you are not willing to get yourself locked into something that is unpleasant or wrong for you as an individual.

Even being a love addict is a positive sign. You are a caring person who wants to give to someone else. The fact that your method was not a good one does not diminish the quality of your effort.

Do you have plants or a pet? Then you are able to care for another life.

Did you go to work on time this morning, do your job, and leave after a full day? Then you have the integrity to be of value to your employer.

Did you disdain work, going in late or not at all and leaving early, if you bothered to show up? That may be a negative in your employer's eyes, but it is positive in the sense that you show you can sometimes take needed time for yourself.

Every aspect of your existence has a positive side to it. You don't have to be handsome or beautiful, sophisticated, wealthy, or the possessor of an expensive, highly desired car in order to think of yourself as having good traits. You simply have to look at life objectively to recognize that you, like everyone else, have good points, and these are what you will list.

Don't worry about what you have always viewed to be your goals in life. Sometimes our dreams are unrealistic. Sometimes "real life" has a way of interfering with our plans. When Jim was a janitor, he wanted to be a rich and famous writer living in Beverly Hills. Eventually he got a job as night man at a small radio station. From there he developed a program interviewing celebrities, giving him the opportunity to collect their autographs. Then he began writing. He got so many assignments that he had no time for the station, and eventually quit his radio job. But he continued to collect autographs.

When Jim was in his thirties, facing the crisis of love addiction and working this program, he tended to focus on what he had *not* done. He was living in a small town, unmarried, and dependent upon a roommate to pay the bills. His income from writing was little above subsistence. He was not in Beverly Hills. He was not doing anything his mother would have approved of when he was growing up the son of alcoholic parents. Yet when Jim worked this program, he found that he was one of only a few hundred full-time freelance writers in the United States.

Jim's positives included the fact that he was working in the field of his dreams. He was not having to take a part-time job. His income was slowly increasing as he gained more understanding of the business. And not only had his hobby brought him regional fame, the value of the autographs turned out to be such that he had unknowingly accumulated a quarter-of-a-million-dollar estate. He wasn't in his Beverly Hills home, but if he liquidated his hobby, he probably could afford one. He was far better than he realized, as he discovered when he made his list.

Make certain you list everything objectively, then look at the list and notice how many entries you have made. Don't compare yourself to anyone else. You will always see yourself as inferior to some, superior to others, when the truth is that we are all very much the same. I have worked with multimillionaires who had very low self-esteem, despite extensive material possessions and a staff of servants. And I have known people who barely survive on minimum wage but who accept themselves, who are happy and content with life. They would like to earn more money, yes—yet they are delighted to be alive, loving, compassionate, honest, regularly reaching out to others regardless of their economic and social status.

Remember how you felt earlier? Remember how you thought you had to gain your identity through your lover or spouse? Now you are beginning to see that you are special, that you do have value for yourself, not because of someone else.

Reinforcing a Positive Self-Image

The series of exercises that follow represent the final stage of the program. Their purpose is to reinforce the positive self-image you are beginning to acquire. These exercises are standard psychological tools used by many therapists to reinforce behavioral change after the individual gains conscious awareness. Some of these exercises I originated and are now used by others. Some of these exercises and/or the concepts used in developing them were created by John Bradshaw, Carl Jung, Milton Erickson, R.D. Laing, and others. The original ideas were generally used alone by their creators, such as Bradshaw's concepts that are the basis for the section on Discovering Unfulfilled Needs you will find. However, I have found that they should be used in combination. In this manner they have proven successful both for emotional trauma and physical training, including training with Olympic and other world-class athletes. They include fractional relaxation—the deliberate relaxation of all parts of the body, resulting in brain wave changes—and visualization techniques to reinforce conscious awareness. These procedures have been used in conjunction with the first part of the program by several thousand people involved with love addiction in my practice, and in the practices of those who use the methods described—always with success.

Beginning: Fractional Relaxation

For this first exercise, fractional relaxation, you will be gradually moving inward, and for this you need to relax completely. Unplug the telephone and turn off the television, the radio, and any other distraction. Then sit on a chair or recline so as to be completely comfortable, your eyes closed. Inhale slowly through your nose, then exhale slowly through your mouth. During the first effort, you may find yourself falling asleep. There is nothing wrong with this. It means that you had more tension than you realized, tension that is now being released. However, the goal is to stay awake and alert to the subconscious world within.

There are two ways to handle this exercise. The first is to read it over, think about it, and then follow it on your own. The second approach is to have a trusted friend or lover talk you through it. Have this person read this section to you, helping you experience everything that will take place. Just make certain the person you select cares about you and will willingly help you take the time to heal. This is not always possible, but when it is, you will find the approach a little easier.

Start with your feet. Let them relax. Feel the tension leave them. They no longer have to convey you from place to place, to hold the weight of your body. They are feeling all the stress of daily wear and tear disappear.

Now let your ankles relax. Again feel the tension fade.

Move on to your legs, your thighs, and your abdomen. Experience your chest becoming almost buoyant as you breathe.

Your body is becoming increasingly relaxed. The problems of the past are of no concern. The worries of the future do not matter.

There is only the present, and you are at peace.

Continue relaxing your shoulders, your arms and hands. Relax your forehead. The lines of tension are disappearing. Your eyelids are comfortably closed, your mind awake but aware that there is nothing to disturb you. Nothing is more important than you and the world within.

Discovering Unfulfilled Needs

Now visualize the house or apartment where you grew up as a child. Take a look all around, noticing that it has not changed at all. If there were trees, they are still there. If there was a flower garden, it is blooming just as it was when you still were playing and going to school. Perhaps you smell the aroma of newly cut grass or the food being prepared in a nearby restaurant. Wherever you lived, city or country, the sounds, the sights, and the smells are there. You have returned as an adult to the place you knew as a child.

Go inside the house and return to the room you had as a little girl or little boy. Take a good look around, because nothing has changed. See where you always slept? The bedding is exactly as you saw it each day. All the furnishings, the decorations, everything you liked or disliked is there.

Now I want you to remember the traumas that you experienced in that house. I want you to remember the unpleasant times, either that you experienced personally or that happened with the others who lived there. Listen to the angry voices, the threats, or whatever else took place. Remember the verbal or emotional violence, the bitter disappointments, the frustrations. You are safe. You are distant. You can remember everything, but you know you are not physically involved. There is no reason to fear. The pain is from the past, and of the past. You are safe, but you are aware.

Now go back to your room. Do you see the child sitting on the bed? This is you, a much younger you. This is you at the age you were when you experienced those traumas. The clothes are what you wore. The shoes are what you wore. The child is you, and he or she recognizes you when you are in the room.

This is your inner child. This is the child who has remained in your subconscious all these years. This is the hurting child who has been reacting to the people in your life, making decisions and acting in a manner appropriate to a child's understanding. This is the child whose unresolved pain has been having such an impact on you that your life has been one of frustrating love relationships.

Now I want you to focus on the needs you had that were not fulfilled by your mother and father. Let your mind and that of the child within become one. Listen to that child and remember all the needs that were never met.

Next, visualize your mother and father as they were then. If you lacked biological parents, visualize whoever was your primary caretaker or caretakers. This might be a single parent, a stepparent and a biological parent, a relative, or a guardian, including foster parents or orphanage personnel. Whichever adults were an intimate part of your life back then are the ones you should be visualizing.

Now I want you to talk to those people. I want you to tell them of your unfulfilled needs.

"Dad," you might say, "you always promised that you would come to my T-ball games, but you never took time off from the office, and I thought you were ashamed of me. I tried to be the best player on the team, but even when I won that trophy, you never went to the ceremony."

"Mom," you might say, "you were never home. You told me I was big enough to get my own dinner, that you had to go out. I know you were doing important things for yourself, and I know I was always silent. But Mom, I needed you to talk with me about school, about relationships, about what was on my mind, and you never did."

Explain every hurt that mattered to you. Let each of them know how you felt, the pain that lingered in your heart.

Hold your inner child's hand, if it will help you. Together you will be overcoming all the trauma you have endured for far too long. That is why it is important that you express all your feelings.

If you are alone, you can speak aloud. If someone is guiding you, you will probably want to do it privately.

Don't worry about the reaction. And don't be concerned if the needs sound childish with the perspective of hindsight. You did not have such a perspective as a child. You only knew what you were experiencing, and you could only understand it with your inner child's awareness. The important thing is to tell them everything.

Once you have finished expressing all the unfulfilled needs you have kept inside for too long, I want you to begin looking at how you have tried to fulfill them through your past relationships. Start with your mother and father or whatever adults were involved with you when you were growing up. Review how you tried to get them to fulfill your needs. Remember all the things you did. They did not work, of course. If they had, you would not be reading this book today. But review in your own mind what you did to try to have your needs met.

Now think of each of your failed relationships. Think about how each relationship involved your attempts to fulfill those needs your parents or other guardians failed to meet.

Remember what you did to get your needs fulfilled with your adult partners. Perhaps you begged or cajoled. Perhaps you were a "nice little girl or boy." You may have tried to do all the right things for the people you were with, pleasing each person if you possibly could. Certainly you repressed your anger, your frustration, your fear, and your pain. You were Daddy's good little girl or boy. You were Mommy's good little girl or boy. You smiled sweetly all the time, never showing any feelings or emotions.

Perhaps you learned not to show emotions at all. Maybe you got your mouth washed out with soap when you showed emotions as a child. Or you experienced the swift, stinging application of a hairbrush or belt to your rear end. Whatever the punishment, you quickly learned that it was safer to repress your needs than to express them.

These unfulfilled needs were brought to each new adult relationship, and again they went unfulfilled. The pain continued, because none of your approaches worked, right up to your most recent relationship.

You did not get your needs met, and look at all the things that you did. Look at all the machinations and maneuvers, and none of them worked. They didn't work when you were a child. They didn't work with your adult relationships in the past. So why should they work now? That is why it is time for a change.

Next I want you to visualize yourself standing with that inner child. Your parents or the people who raised you are no longer in the room. It is just you and that inner child, the boy or girl you were when growing up, the one who has been unfulfilled for so long.

Tell that inner child you love him/her. Tell the inner child that you will fulfill those inner needs. You will give the inner child the love that was never received. You will provide the attention he or she deserves. You will provide the acceptance that was never given. You will give the praise so richly earned yet seldom experienced.

Ask your inner child to open to you, to allow you to love her or him. Then do it. Hold the inner child or just talk as you feel comfortable. Express your love, your caring, your desire to give the inner child the happiness that should have been a birthright, the normal experience of childhood, not the rare exception in the formative years of existence. You will give your inner child the love he or she never received. You will provide the praise so richly deserved, yet that never occurred. You will notice his or her achievements, taking pride in the inner child's existence.

Your parents didn't do that, so subconsciously, as an adult, you tried to gain what you missed as a child from the relationships you have experienced. Yet the men or women you tried to love as an adult could not fulfill the needs of your inner child. They just helped you to create a co-dependent personality.

Now you can start to break those walls down. You can have a relationship that exists for its own sake, not a fantasy relationship created in a desperate move to ease the hurt of your past. You can start to get rid of love addiction.

Are you doing this? Are you accepting yourself? Are you giving yourself the love you wanted as a child but didn't get? The praise you wanted as a child but didn't get? The attention you wanted as a child but didn't get?

This is the core of what it means to be a love slave. You are *not* addicted to your mother or father. You are not trying to recreate the person who denied you through your relationships. Instead, you are addicted to having your needs fulfilled because they were never fulfilled as a child. Yet you cannot get your childhood *needs* fulfilled through a healthy, constructive adult relationship. All you are doing is forming a co-dependent personality.

Hold your inner child close to you. Tell your inner child of your love. Tell your inner child that you will never, never abandon him/her. You will always be there for him/her. You will always love him/her. He/she is very special to you.

Tell your inner child, "There is nothing wrong with you at all. It is not your fault that your parents didn't fulfill your needs, didn't love you as you deserved to be loved, didn't accept you. It wasn't your fault that they verbally abused one another. It wasn't your fault that your mother was beaten up by your father, or that your father was attacked by your mother. It wasn't your fault that your father or mother drank too much. No matter what happened to you or around you as a child, it wasn't your fault. You had no control, and there is no reason to feel any shame about it. You were good. Any mistakes that you made came from being young, from being like every other girl or boy your age. You weren't a bad child. You were good." Say, "I'm very proud of you, my precious inner child."

Reclaim your inner child. Take as long as you like to share your feelings with your him/her. Love that inner child.

You are still in the house where you grew up. Your inner child is still there too, though the two of you have bonded with one another. Your parents or any other adults who raised you are also there, only now you are present, the adult you, the friend of your inner child. You will be your inner child's advocate and protector.

Allow your inner child to tell your parents, "I'm angry with you! I'm angry with you! I'm angry with you!" Then have your inner child tell the adults why. Explain the needs that were not fulfilled and encourage your inner child to tell your parents that their failure was unjust.

You did everything to get your needs fulfilled. You did everything to get them to give you the love you deserved. But they didn't do it, and their failure screwed up your life.

Say "I'm angry with you. I did everything to get you to love me, and you didn't love me. I'm angry with you for that." Tell your father you're angry with him for the physical abuse of your mother. And tell your mother you're angry with her for the abuse of your father. Whatever the pain you endured, tell them about it. Tell them you are angry about it. Tell them that it should not have happened, that they had no right to hurt each other. To hurt you.

Tell them, "I'm angry with you because you didn't praise me."

Tell them, "I'm angry with you because you haven't fulfilled my needs."

This is not selfishness on your part. No child asks to be born. A single act of sexual intercourse is all that is needed to create a child, whereas parenting requires adults to make a loving, selfless commitment. An infant is totally depending upon his or her parents for physical survival. From birth until they are old enough to be out on their own, children are totally dependent upon their parents for emotional support.

The ability to love starts with one's relationship with the primary-care adults. The child must be nurtured. The child must learn to explore, to crawl, to walk, to run, to test the limits in life. Parents earn trust. Parents gain love only by so loving that child that their love is ultimately reflected in the child's response. We cannot imitate what we fail to experience.

Your parents owed you everything when you were a child. This does not mean material possessions. No one ever caused long-term pain by saying no to a Barbie doll, an electric train, a video game, or any other toy. I have never had a patient come to me to heal as a result of his parents' refusal to buy a stereo, a color television set, or an expensive sports car for the child's sixteenth birthday. A loved child raised in poverty has wealth beyond price. An un-loved or underloved child raised with riches has a poverty of the soul that a king's ransom cannot end.

A parent is required by the laws in all fifty of the United States to supply the means for a child's physical survival. A parent must adequately feed, clothe, and house the child, but there is no law that says a parent has to give love. When love is not experienced, however, or when intimacy means pain, the parent has failed.

Your inner child is not angry because a Christmas wish list went unfulfilled. Your inner child has forgotten all about the desire for a tricycle that caused a temper tantrum in the middle of the toy store. Your inner child does not remember the anger when Mom said "no" to a board game "every other kid in school" was getting. Your inner child may be five years old and hurting deeply because of traumas at that time, but he or she has the maturity to understand the difference between emotional needs and the "wants" of normal childhood self-centered greed.

Some psychologists say we have no right to blame our parents for problems we may have after we leave home. They say that parents are the unfair targets of people too weak to find their own way in the world.

This criticism is not valid in the case of love addicts. Certainly there are adults who refuse to take responsibility for their own actions. They are always looking to blame someone else. They are like the soldier who says, "I was just following orders," or the bureaucrat who says, "If it's not in my rule book, it can't be done." They are people who never want to admit that they have power and influence, that they can stand alone and be responsible.

Such people are not your inner child. Your inner child has no awareness of selfishness. Your inner child is not a bureaucrat or a soldier. Your inner child is a fragile, honest, open being, capable of telling the truth and sensing reality. What your inner child is saying in this exercise cannot be denied.

Of course there may have been extenuating circumstances. Of course you, as an adult, might one day look objectively at every aspect of your parents' situation. You might find that, as one adult for another, you have compassion for some of the problems that they were experiencing. However, if they failed the child you were, if they failed you in the ways that matter to everyone, then in those instances they were wrong. And it is those instances, and those instances alone, that you are healing now. This exercise brings out what is important to all children, and this exercise is crucial for your healing.

The anger you are letting your inner child express to your parents or the other adults who raised you is based on their failure to love. It is based on their failure to nurture you effectively. It is based on their unwillingness to meet emotional needs as important for your health as adequate food and clothing.

Ultimately, a child can learn to survive by ordering out for pizza when his or her mother and father stay away from home. A child cannot call a stranger to get love. And as an adult, until your inner child is healed, you cannot openly, honestly, and wholly give what you failed to receive.

Your inner child has a righteous anger. He or she is not being selfish. Your inner child is recognizing his or her inherent goodness, inherent value, inherent right to the happiness of a parent's unconditional love. That is why you should take your time as you go through this series of exercises, and get the healthy anger out.

The two emotions that freeze you in childhood are fear and anger. Fear is not a factor right now, but anger is. And as the adult protector of your inner child, you must remind that inner child that it is all right to be angry. Your parents can no longer cause pain. Your inner child is in charge, letting out all the tightly held feelings.

Inhale deeply. Exhale slowly. Inhale. Exhale. The emotions have been intense, and now it is time to go to a different phase of this exercise.

You have acted out your anger inappropriately over the years. I know this, because everyone who has found himself or herself addicted to a love object has acted in the same manner. It is time to look over your life and see what you did and when you did it.

Now start reviewing your adult life. Let the adult in you see where you have vented your anger inappropriately. This may have meant displacing your anger on your boyfriend, girlfriend, lover, or spouse. It may have been an employer, a same-level coworker, or an employee. Perhaps it was in your business dealings, such as with your landlord or a shop clerk. Perhaps it was with a family member who experienced totally unwarranted wrath.

Whatever the case, review each instance as you remember it. Because it was inappropriate, even though you were unable to stop yourself, you may have felt a twinge of discomfort for what you were doing. You may have thought to yourself, "I know I'm over-reacting, but . . ." You may have been reminded by a friend or even the object of your anger that you were taking matters out of proportion. What should have been a minor annoyance became an intense explosion.

Or you may just have had an underlying feeling of discomfort. Perhaps someone has long made you uncomfortable. Perhaps there is someone with whom you do not wish to have a relationship. Perhaps you have felt that there is no reason to dislike a certain person, yet you just can't seem to stop yourself. You don't know why. You don't really think about it. Yet he or she has always seemed to be someone who just "rubs you the wrong way."

Whatever the case, review these times of inappropriate anger. These were the times you were angry with your mother and father. Inappropriate anger comes from your needs not being fulfilled by the primary relationship you had as a child.

I say your mother and father, though the same goes for foster parents, stepparents, or any other adult caretakers. So long as you have anger over your unfulfilled needs, you are going to be stuck in love-addicted relationships. Love addiction cannot end while you remain angry over unfulfilled needs. It is impossible for you to have a long-term, healthy, monogamous, totally committed relationship with anyone so long as you are stuck in that primary relationship you experienced as a child. So long as you are living at least a part of your life in the past, then you can never be totally in the present for someone else.

Your relationship to the past is a little like having one foot cemented to the ground. You have full range of motion with every other part of your body. You can swing your free leg, wave your arms, flex your wrists, type, make a sandwich, and handle all bodily functions. But you will not be able to move forward, backward, or side to side except to the degree allowed by the one free leg. A part of you is riveted in the same spot until that glue can be removed.

You may find that the angry incidents are limited to a small number of events connected with each of your attempts at establishing intimate relationships. You may find that the incidents are numerous. Take your time as you work through this exercise, and repeat this process as you repeat this entire section over the next few days.

Now return to looking at your inner child. Tell the inner child that he or she is loved and accepted. Explain that you will always be there to provide love, advocacy, friendship, and support. You will fulfill all of your inner child's needs. He or she is very special to you. He or she is deeply, unconditionally loved.

Now have your inner child put his or her arms around you as the two of you embrace. Hold each other close. Feel each other's hearts. Feel that warm sense of integration as you happily hold one another.

When you both feel safe and comforted, walk with your inner child past your parents. Walk out the door of the house you were in as a child, holding your inner child's hand. If you lived in an apartment, then the two of you should walk out the door together, taking the steps or elevator to leave the building.

Your parents are not coming with you. Your parents remain in the home where you were raised, where you experienced those traumas, where you confronted them and the past in the exercise you have just been doing.

Walk down the long street of years. If it is easier, carry your inner child in your arms. The two of you will be covering the time from your past and your present, and though the way seems long, because you are touching one another, you do not grow tired. Instead, you are happy and refreshed, you and your inner child, walking up to Now, to this moment in time, the pain of the past so far back you can no longer see your parents (or other primary caretakers).

When you reach the present moment, allow you and your inner child to integrate. Feel the two of you becoming one. No longer will the inner child be scared, hurting, and alone. The adult You has blended with your inner child. He or she is no longer at risk, no longer unfulfilled. The adult You is complete.

Finally, take the time to review the incidents of the past once again, from childhood to the present, looking at how you have attempted to get your unfulfilled needs satisfied in your different relationships. This will not take long, because you already have so much understanding.

Once you have done this, think about why you chose the relationships you selected over the years. Look at the characteristics of the men or women you chose to try to love as you attempted to have your unfulfilled needs satisfied in each new relationship. What were their personalities? Were they like the personality of your mother? Your father? Some other primary caretaker?

Why did you choose them? They had to have some similarity with your mother or father's make-up. Think about what that similarity may have been.

That is what I want you to focus on. This is where you change the pattern of the past. When you understand this, you will see why you have made the decisions you have made in selecting potential partners.

Take this new understanding and ask yourself, "Are these my needs right now?" They were your needs when you were seven or eight or nine. They were your needs when you were passing through the various stages of childhood. But are these your needs right now? Or are your needs different? And what is that difference?

Ask yourself, "Are you addicted to those unfulfilled needs?" I think you will find that you are, for this is the core of love addiction.

Now review in your mind your addiction to those unfulfilled needs, from the time they were unfulfilled as a child until now. Let yourself be aware of your addiction to those needs.

Finally, consider how this has affected your self-image, because it has. Your addiction to unfulfilled needs has molded you into the person you have tried to be. The addiction has not cast you in stone. You are not a statue whose shape cannot be altered. Instead, you exist like the first shaping of still-soft clay. The form is evident, but a gentle hand can alter the contours of your existence, restoring you to the kind of person you want to be, should be, and can be.

Your addiction has given you a needy self-image. It has given you the self-image of someone in pursuit of an impossible goal. You are trying to find in an intimate relationship someone who will fulfill the needs you had when you still were in the care of your mother, father, or other adult. But only they were capable of fulfilling those needs when you were a child, and they never did and they never will. Now, as an independent adult, you are repeatedly setting yourself up for failure.

You have what could be called an addictive self-image. You have turned to *things* to try and anesthetize yourself. Perhaps you have involved yourself in drugs or alcohol, in sex, in anorexia, bulimia, or overeating. You may have become a compulsive shopper or gambler. You may have been promiscuous or sexually frigid, unable to enjoy normal relationships within a committed living arrangement.

See how all of this has served as the mold for you. The person you have tried to be is usually negative. And if your life, to others, has been a positive one, there are usually reasons for your actions that should not have to exist.

For example, you may be a constant pleaser, accepting any volunteer task on the job or in your church, synagogue, social organization, or other group. You might be the good little girl or boy, doing whatever you think will give the other person pleasure. You might be helpful at all times, friendly, and willing to extend yourself under any circumstance, even when one less commitment, one more hour of rest, might be best for you.

There is nothing wrong with doing good works. However, when they are done to try for a response related to the unfulfilled needs of your inner child, this is not a healthy situation. There is a better way for you to live, but the approach you have taken seems so productive to an outsider, you are rarely encouraged to modify your behavior.

Remember that *what* you do is not the concern here. It is *why* you do it. Discovering that you are doing good works for others in order to please a parent does not mean that you will stop doing such works. It just means that you will be motivated in the future by the personal pleasure you get from the actions themselves. You will no longer be motivated by the negative pleasures from your past.

The same is true with your interpersonal relationships. You may still find yourself drawn to the same kind of person, only now you will accept that person for what he or she is instead of projecting a fantasy on that person.

We all tend to deify our parents. At birth we are totally dependent upon them for survival. Food, shelter, and personal hygiene are all outside our control. Before we can roll over on our backs, before we can propel our bodies very far in any direction, before we can hold a bottle or a fork, go to the toilet or clean ourselves, our parents are handling our needs. They are all-powerful, all-capable. They are to the infant a little like God the Creator to that which has been created.

We don't wish to lose that special awareness as we get older, though it is only natural that we do. We learn to get our own food. We learn to put on extra clothing to keep warm, or remove layers of clothing to cool our bodies. We go to the bathroom by ourselves. We bathe without assistance. And we can travel abour our neighborhoods unaided. Yet still the words and actions of our parents are essential to our emotional health. We delight in their approval and are deeply hurt by their disapproval. We learn their flaws, yet deny those flaws exist. We blame ourselves for the failings they have always had, yet which we could not comprehend as dependent newborns.

The exercise series you have just completed does more than give you self-awareness and restore control, it also removes the fantasy from the parent/child relationship. You realize the very human qualities of your parents. You see their flaws, accepting them as you accept their strengths. You respect the good while not being shocked by the bad. You avoid nothing, accept everything, and develop a whole relationship.

Then, as you heal through this understanding, no longer having an inner child frozen in the past, you can begin to look objectively at your current relationships. You can begin to understand the person you have been dating or to whom you are married for who that person is, not who you wanted him or her to be.

Can Your Present Relationship Survive?

After working the program I have just discussed, Herb realized that his marriage to Naomi was over. She had given up on him by the time he came for therapy. She was tired of trying to get him to see her as a person with wants, needs, and qualities worthy of respect. She was tired of feeling like a dressmaker's dummy for his romantic fantasies. She told him that in order for them to continue, one of them would have to move out. Then they would have to court, getting to know each other in ways he had previously never allowed. At that time they would know whether there was any chance they could relate. She also said that doing that no longer seemed to be worth the effort. She would rather start fresh with someone else, a situation to which he agreed.

Herb began looking to women he enjoyed as companions for his love interest. He developed a relationship with Moira, a delightful woman with a brilliant mind, a sparkling sense of humor, and a body that could charitably be described as "plain." Yet because he let himself know the real woman, he discovered that she was actually a loving, caring individual who took great pleasure in sex with him. By looking past the physical appearance, he finally had the true happiness he had been frustrated in seeking over the years.

Does this mean that by working the program to end your love addiction, you will also be ending your marriage or love affair? Not necessarily.

Not all love-addicted relationships are alike. Some involve a love object who also has emotional problems, though usually not the same as his partner. Typical is the narcissist who is totally enraptured with himself. The narcissist perceives himself as being at the center of the universe, ignoring or disdaining the lover or spouse. The narcissist believes that he or she is the high point of perfection, and takes the fawning of the love addict as being right and proper. No matter how friendly or nice the narcissist may seem, the person actually feeds on the problems of the other, a no-win situation for a healthy relationship. Unless the narcissist is willing to seek therapy, the relationship is doomed when the love addict completes the program. For the first time in years, the love addict has a valid sense of self-worth and will not tolerate the destructive antics of the partner. It is only during those rare occasions when both partners find themselves at a low point simultaneously that the narcissist is likely to seek therapy, then agree to explore the marriage.

In most instances the relationship can be saved. Overcoming your love addiction enables you to cope with the other aspects of your life. You are now able to communicate with your spouse or lover. You are able to put yourself in that person's position, to understand the pain that was caused by your problem.

Talk freely with your partner. Ask him or her to read this book so that he or she can understand your past. You will be amazed at the relief that occurs. At last she will have a grasp of what had previously been a highly troubling impasse in her attempts to build her relationship with you.

Next explain that you would like to get to know her, not as a fantasy but as a whole human being. Admit that you may be scared. Admit that your failure to observe objectively in the past means that you are essentially intimate strangers. Admit that you know your actions have been painful and that a fresh courtship, one where you are truly open to each other, may yet prolong the pain because of all the weeks, months, or years when you fled from reality.

Then stress that you feel that the relationship is worth trying to save. Say that you are willing to do whatever it takes to truly get to know each other.

In almost every instance, the person who was the love object is willing to take the emotional gamble involved. The courtship that results often brings about the greatest happiness either person has known in years. It is a mature romance, born from adversity that, having survived the pain, can result in a mutual vulnerability that brings true joy. Nothing is ever the same again, but the newness is all positive. And so long as each party is willing to work at building the relationship to an ever-greater degree, the effort frequently results in a lifelong commitment.

Eleanor made a discovery after she worked the program. She was involved with Nathan, a pharmacist she had been dating for more than a year, and she had been trying to please him. Although they were neither living together nor engaged, she spent her days trying to take care of him. She was an artist's representative who showed her clients' work to various advertising agencies, galleries, and other locations where they might make sales. As a result, she could create her own hours to a great degree, which she did.

Each work day, Eleanor stopped by Nathan's pharmacy with a hot lunch she had purchased at one of the carry-out places in the area. Each evening she tried to arrange to cook for him, either in his apartment or her own. If he went out for the evening with someone else, she would walk his dog. When his telephone went out, she shuffled her appointments so that she could remain in his home until the repair person arrived.

Nathan never asked for her help in this way. There were times when he seemed annoyed by what he called her "incessant mothering." As much as he appreciated the thought behind it all, he was frustrated by it. "I like getting out after the noon rush, walking to the park, and buying a sandwich from a vendor sometimes," he said. "And Frank, the superintendent in my building, will walk my dog when I can't get home on time. I tip him a few bucks and he's happy. Sometimes I just like to feel I can be spontaneous during the week."

Eleanor would hear none of that. She "knew" what he really wanted and needed. He wanted consistency in his life. He wanted someone who cared for him, who respected his lifestyle and helped him lead it more comfortably. She knew that his occasional dates with other women were casual, that he was not having sex with them, and she was right. What she did not understand was that he liked the thought of occasionally being the pursuer instead of feeling like he was married without being married, trapped in an emotional cage of someone else's creation.

After working the program, Eleanor remembered her own childhood. Her father was a rising corporate executive who worked long days and traveled frequently during the week. Her mother had too much money to consider taking a job, yet too much time on her hands to stay at home. She became active in various volunteer groups. She also had a few women friends in similar financial and social circumstances who liked to play cards, go drinking at the country club, and generally pass the time of day together.

Eleanor was old enough not to need a sitter, yet too young to be alone as much as her mother left her. The cleaning woman and gardener handled their respective tasks, neither trying to be nor expected to be a surrogate mother.

"Can't you be here when I come home for lunch?" Eleanor asked her mother. "Can't we have dinner together when Daddy's out of town?" She had friends from school who lacked her family's income and growing prestige who seemed to be much closer together. When she was invited to their homes, lunch was hot soup and a freshly made sandwich, not cold pizza and a glass of milk. Dinner was a lovingly made meal, hot and plentiful, even if inexpensive. Always her friends' parents were together, and if they couldn't be, at least their mothers were home with them.

"When I was in seventh grade, I learned how to cook in school," Eleanor told me. "I decided that I would show Mommy how much I loved her, how much she would enjoy getting to know me. I went to the grocery store when I got my allowance and I bought everything I knew how to prepare. I got macaroni and cheese, some canned vegetables, and a few other things. It was a pretty terrible mix, but these were all things I could do myself.

"Then I took the best china I knew wasn't reserved for special occasions and fixed the table for us. Daddy was in Milwaukee that week, so there were just the two of us. But I went all out, including stealing some flowers from a neighbor's yard to use as a centerpiece. I was going to use our own, but I thought that might not be special enough.

"I had this fantasy of my mother seeing what I had done and being overwhelmed with love. I thought she would change her habits and start spending more time with me. Instead, she never came home. I was expecting her around five, and had everything so it would be ready when she came in the door. Then I put on the dress I wore to Sunday school, sat down and waited. She didn't come.

"I tried to not eat anything, but I got too hungry. I kept nibbling at everything, trying to keep it looking nice as I did. Six o'clock came. Then seven. Finally she came breezing in at seven-thirty, apologizing to me and saying she got caught up in a 'hot Mah Jongg game' at the club. She told me she was glad I had fixed myself something because she had eaten at the club and was really too tired to bother.

"She never expressed surprise at what I did. She never expressed pleasure. I don't think she really noticed anything different. I was just shattered."

The adult Eleanor's inner child had long felt rejected. She had made the subconscious decision to do for Nathan what was never done for her. She projected her need for closeness, for someone intensely caring each day, onto a man who had no such concerns. She was treating him in a way that would have met the needs of her own inner child, then couldn't understand why he wasn't overwhelmed with love.

"He found my actions to be too extreme for his needs and wants," Eleanor told me. "And I resented him for it. I thought he was rejecting me just like my mother did, though at least he was staying around to eat what I prepared. He always thanked me. He always appreciated the gesture. And he constantly tried to explain why he would prefer that I not go to so much trouble.

"To me, holding back was refusing him love. He worried that I would completely smother him if we became more involved with each other. Yet until I looked back on my unfulfilled needs through working the program, I resented what I saw as his callousness toward my loving actions."

It is very hard to have a relationship with someone when you can't see him or hear him, when he is nothing more than the projection of the father and/or mother who failed to meet your needs. The body is different. The voice is different. The mind is different. Yet you are focusing on a limited number of characteristics, then sealing the rest of that person, his or her very essence, inside an impregnable container. You are not sharing a life, have not shared one, and will not share one until the healing is complete.

A healthy relationship comes only when two people come together, each with a positive self image. This does not mean being self-centered. Instead, they are comfortable with themselves, their strengths, their weaknesses, their goals, and the realities of life. They have mutual respect, wanting to share all aspects of a life without smothering one another, manipulating one another, or needing the other to feel whole. It is their ability to lead independent, healthy, happy lives that enables them to achieve a loving relationship with each other. Their love is for the whole person, accepting that which is different, never fearing loss, always willing to grow because each knows the other will never make unrealistic requests.

Eleanor was not acting out of love for Nathan. Eleanor was doing for Nathan what she had so desperately wanted her mother to do for her. Partially frozen in the past, she could not see Nathan for himself, even though he respected and loved who she was more completely than she imagined.

Before working this program, Darwin became emotionally withdrawn whenever his wife Dorothy was upset at the breakfast table. There were no other problems throughout the day that affected him in the same way. For example, there was the time Dorothy had an unusually difficult night. She worked overtime at the office, not taking the time for dinner although she was hypoglycemic. She had developed a terrible headache by the time she ate, and though she took some aspirin, it never quite went away. She was annoyed with herself, because she knew better than to delay eating like that, yet had not used her better judgment.

That evening, Dorothy had tried to install some book shelves in a corner of the apartment where she and Darwin lived. She had made such installations in other places where they lived in the past, never realizing that those walls were different. They had been solid, whereas the current apartment had dry wall. She could only put the weight-bearing screws into studs, something she discovered only after the shelving, partially filled with books, went crashing to the floor, taking portions of the dry wall with them.

Everything seemed to be going wrong before she went to bed, and she was feeling sorry for herself, angry over her mistakes. Then, the next morning, when she went to make breakfast, she accidentally dropped a carton of eggs, breaking two of them. It was the last straw. She cursed herself, cursed the eggs, and angrily said, "I might as well give up. I'm worthless around here. I can't do anything right."

Darwin froze as if in terror when Dorothy started cursing. Tears came to her eyes, but he did not try to comfort her or even help clean up the mess on the floor. He emotionally closed down, wanting only to scream at her or run away. He went into the bathroom, closed the door, then sat on the toilet, trying to read the newspaper so his mind would not be on the woman he loved.

Dorothy was angry that he was hiding. "The least you could

do is help me," she told him, crying. "I'm doing a really shitty job of helping myself."

Darwin did help clean up the broken eggs. Then he drank a glass of juice, and said he had to leave right away or he'd be late for work. He was actually an hour early, something they both realized, but neither quite understood his exaggerated behavior.

Eventually Darwin faced his love addiction and tried the exercises you have been learning. He remembered that breakfast during his childhood was the only time the entire family was together, and his parents used it as the time for dealing with everything unpleasant. Scoldings were meted out for various infractions of family rules that had taken place the day before. Anger over work was vented, and so was frustration over financial problems. It was a time of tension and acting out with verbal rage, which Darwin hated.

Dorothy's quite-normal reaction to a set of unpleasant circumstances was no problem. The difficulty came when, in Darwin's subconscious mind, Dorothy stopped being Darwin's wife and became, instead, his mother. He did not see Dorothy's face when she was angry at breakfast; he saw his mother. He did not hear Dorothy's voice; he heard his mother's. And he was not a grown man in control of his life. He was the little child seeking to flee the violence and anger.

Darwin was not emotionally disturbed. He did not project his mother's face onto Dorothy's when they made love. He was not having a fantasy incestuous relationship. Instead, he was experiencing his inner child's reaction to an experience that instantly sent him psychologically into the past.

Working the program, Darwin found that he could accept his life as it was. He no longer expected his parents to fulfill his needs. He knew that was impossible. He knew that what they failed to do when he was growing up would also not occur as an adult.

By integrating with his inner child, Darwin could keep his current relationship in perspective. He explained the problem to Dorothy, who was part understanding, part resentful. She said that it hurt that he could not be living with her in the present. At the same time, she had noticed his overreacting to her temper and said that she would try to control her emotions more.

The arrangement took time. Everyone has to express anger, and Dorothy was no exception. There were still instances when Darwin reacted inappropriately and she overreacted in response, shouting at him that she wanted the right to express herself. "Can't I be angry? Dorothy? Your wife? Can't I lose my temper? You lose yours, Darwin. You curse all the time and you don't see me withdrawing. I accept your need or tell you that you're being an ass. But I don't emotionally curl into a fetal position like you do!"

Darwin knew she was right. Though changing was hard, the healing that began with the exercises reached the point where, though he still didn't like Dorothy's being upset in the morning, he knew it was Dorothy being upset. "I understood the here and now. I was no longer living in the past," he told me. "I stopped confusing Dorothy and my mother's actions in childhood. I focused on why I loved her. I thought about the things she did that I didn't like about her, that I wouldn't like about anyone. I weighed all aspects of the relationship and became so aroused by the thoughts of the good, I seduced her in the middle of breakfast, something we hadn't done since we first got married. We were both late for work that day, and we were both grinning like Cheshire cats, but it was worth it.

"Dorothy told me that she had considered divorce for a while. She told me that she loved me but couldn't stand the feeling that I wasn't fully with her emotionally.

"All of that has changed, Dr. Green. Life is wonderful in the here and now."

Chapter 9

Nutrition and Exercise

Working the seven steps to healing is essential, but it is not enough for some love slaves. You may find that you have been depressed for so long that you need extra assistance to reinforce the program you have been working. Yet the reason for the depression may not be strictly psychological. Most people who have been in an obsessive love situation actually need to attend to their neglected bodies, exactly as do those who have been involved with stimulant or depressant addiction. This attention involves a modification of diet and exercise, as well as occasional psychological reinforcement exercises.

Examining Your Health

Because you have focused solely on your love object, there is a likelihood that you have ignored your own health. Many love slaves have a tendency to grab quick meals, such as fast food carry-outs, so they can spend more time with the love object. They tend to spend their time either working or pursuing the person they desire. They are constantly experiencing intense emotional stress, and they rely solely on the feelings they receive from the love object in order to relax.

The first step in reinforcing change is to recognize that you cannot love another person if you cannot first love yourself. I don't mean the kind of narcissistic self-love you read about in chapter 8; I am talking about caring for your physical and emotional needs so that you can interact as a whole being. I am talking about creating an environment for yourself that assures that you are in the best possible health.

The following program assumes that you are in good physical health. You are not suffering from a chronic condition that requires special medication. You are not someone who has a natural chemical imbalance such as exists for a manic/depressive, whose body fails to produce lithium salts. And you have not just experienced an emotional trauma, such as the death of a loved one, or physical trauma, such as open-heart surgery, for which a period of depression is natural.

There are no circumstances under which any aspect of the reinforcement program will hurt you; it will work regardless of your age, sex, or physical condition. However, you may find that you either have special needs or do not require the extra effort because your problem is directly related to some other circumstance. If you have any questions, check with your doctor. The program for reinforcement in this chapter is not meant to be a substitute for routine medical care. It is a safe, effective supplement to the steps you have just completed. It was created because of requests from former patients, and I use it here because it has worked for all of them. But it will not counter a preexisting medical condition for which other treatment is necessary.

Step 1: Reducing Sugar

Sugar is the leading cause of depression among otherwise healthy individuals. The way in which your body handles sugar assures that you will either have to be a sugar junkie, constantly consuming small quantities of the substance in candy, coffee, soft drinks, and similar sources, or suffer constant highs and lows throughout the day.

To understand sugar, it is first necessary to understand whole foods. A whole food is any substance that contains all the nutritional factors needed to metabolize itself. If nutrients not supplied by whatever you eat are needed for proper metabolism, then you are not eating a whole food.

All food grown for human consumption is a whole food when first pulled from the ground or plucked from a tree. Eat a carrot, some broccoli, or even just-picked sugar cane and you will be consuming something that is good for your body. All other fruits and vegetables can be obtained (grown or purchased) in their natural state. They may be altered through special processing, such as when sugar is added to canned vegetables, but if eaten either fresh or frozen *without* addition of sugar or syrup, they are nutritious. Whole sugar cane, of course, is rarely sold in stores. It is processed to one degree or another, and that processing destroys the B-complex vitamins needed for full metabolism.

The B-complex vitamins needed to process sugar are obtained either through supplements, if the person chooses to do so, or from body organs rich in B-complex—usually the latter situation, which is one of the reasons heart disease is so prevalent in the United States. Sugar is used extensively in products ranging from catsup to cola drinks, canned vegetables to syrup-packed canned fruit. When processed sugar cane is not used, sugar may be added in the form of corn syrup, fructose, and sucrose. All require extra B-complex vitamins.

One of the major problems with sugar is the way it fools the body. Eat a piece of candy and the sugar signals your pancreas that you have just eaten a big meal. The pancreas responds as it always does when you sit down for serious eating—it releases a large quantity of insulin to metabolize what it thinks might be meat, vegetables, a salad, bread, or whatever else you normally consume.

It would be easy to think that the pancreas is not very bright, that it should know better than to mistake a piece of hard candy for a four-course meal, but the fact is that real foods give off the same signals. Cheese, beef, and other foods all contain small quantities of natural sugars, which serve the function of signaling the pancreas to release the insulin needed for metabolism.

When the insulin is released to handle candy, a sweet roll, cookie, brownie, piece of pie, cake, or other sugar-laden delight, it handles whatever you have eaten, then begins looking around the body for the rest of the meal. You feel a rush, your body more alert. You return to your desk able to do more work.

The problem is that the insulin is still trying to find the meal that you did not consume. It marches through your blood stream, checking every corner of your body's metabolic system, as though in a game of hide-and-seek where the child who is "it" tries to find the other players long after they have gotten bored and gone home.

Such an effort is exhausting biochemically. Your blood sugar drops to next to nothing. You become hungry, lightheaded, and unable to think clearly, but you likely do not go get a meal. You probably go to the vending machine for a candy bar and a cup of coffee. A rush of sugar restores your vitality, the pancreas releases more insulin, and the uneven chase of sugar and insulin resumes again.

This problem of constantly shifting levels of blood sugar and insulin will occur every two to four hours throughout the day. It can be avoided by having two or three full meals each day, depending upon what your body needs, and snacks like cheese, peanut butter, fruit, and nuts.

Cigarette smokers have the same problem, which is one of the reasons it is difficult to quit smoking without increasing caloric intake. Along with the problem of nicotine addiction is that of the sugar used to cure the tobacco. The smoke you inhale contains enough sugar that your body treats cigarettes in a manner similar to candy.

The proof is easy to see. Watch someone who is a casual smoker, not a chain smoker. Notice how roughly every two to three hours after smoking a cigarette, the person feels they "need" another one. The person may reach for it automatically, or may become restless, irritable, and unable to concentrate, excusing himself or herself to go to a smoking area. This pattern is the same as the person's metabolic rate for handling sugar. The candy many people take while giving up smoking is effective, not because they need something in their mouths but because they need the sugar. It is not an oral craving or sucking motion most smokers seek in addition to the nicotine jolt; it is sugar. However, even that craving is stopped by eating whole foods that slowly release natural sugar, such as cheese and meat.

Eventually the pancreas has problems with the sugar/insulin chase. Chronic low-blood-sugar problems (hypoglycemia) may arise, and from that, diabetes.

For the love addict, the emotional trauma of unresolved childhood anger is often reinforced with a poor diet. "I can't do anything right. I 'need' the cola drink to get me through the day. I 'need' my cigarette and/or candy/pie/cake to keep going." Not only are you creating body chemistry problems that contribute to the depression you already have from being a love slave, you make it harder to reinforce the recovery program, since some of the depression never leaves. That residual depression may be the result of sugar, not emotions affected by outside individuals.

Step 2: Adjusting Body Chemistry

Acetylcholine

Acetylcholine is another concern for the recovering love addict. This is your body's neurotransmitter, the chemical that assures healthy, properly functioning nerve synapses in the central nervous system. It is sometimes called "brain sugar," and people who have experienced an LSD trip know what it can do to them. LSD robs the brain of acetylcholine, a fact that results in the so-called "trip." Deadlier is the loss of acetylcholine found in the brains of Alzheimer patients. This loss is what causes, at least in part, the confusion and memory loss of the Alzheimer sufferer. What is not known, at this writing, is whether the lack of acetylcholine precedes or results from the disease.

Love addicts who become lax in their diets are frequently lacking in acetylcholine. As you have difficulty with a relationship, fixing a proper meal does not seem worth the trouble, and you are likely to eat less or binge on junk food. When you are upset over your ongoing relationship problems, bothering to cook or do more than grab a hamburger and fries may seem too big an effort. You receive too little acetylcholine, resulting in symptoms such as drowsiness, confusion, and minor forgetfulness. Then you tell yourself that you are just upset because of difficulties with your relationship. And your friends reinforce this attitude, because the symptoms you are experiencing are identical to those encountered when mourning a relationship loss.

The other problem with insufficient acetylcholine is that there is a tendency to focus on the negative and exaggerate problems. This has been shown as far back as infancy. Acetylcholine is a natural component of lecithin, and lecithin is found in human mothers' milk. Lecithin is *not* found in cows' milk. Children who nurse from their mothers' breasts are calmer when young than children who are bottle-fed using cow's milk. Adults with adequate acetylcholine have an easier time healing from love addiction while working this program.

There are two ways to be certain you have adequate acetylcholine. One is through B-complex vitamin supplement (note that the label information will usually refer to "choline," not the longer "acetylcholine"; these are the same). Such supplements are sold wherever vitamins are available. Research has found that B-complex vitamin supplements work best when the quantities of the vitamins they contain are consistent. You will find many manufacturers package them as B-25 or B-50 or some other designation. This means that the same number of milligrams or micrograms, depending upon the particular B-vitamin, will be a part of the total tablet. Other forms of B-complex vitamins have uneven amounts, and some researchers feel that they are not quite so effective. The different packaging actually relates to the cost to the manufacturer. However, when B-complex vitamins are taken individually rather than in combination, relative amounts do not seem to matter.

The other advantage to the B-complex vitamins is that they are water soluble. This means that any excess you consume will be released in your urine instead of accumulating to what might otherwise be a toxic level.

What are the natural sources of choline? The vitamin is found in egg yolks, fish, soybeans, legumes, organ meats, wheat germ, brewer's yeast, and lecithin. Lecithin, which is sold as a supplement, has a nutty flavor and is good sprinkled on food.

Norepinephrine

When food protein—meat, cheese, beans, etc.—is broken down by enzymes, they form amino acids. If you eat a proper diet, the amino acid phenylalanine will combine with the amino acid tyrosine created by the metabolizing of the food proteins. Those two amino acids, in combination, form norepinephrine.

I realize that these words are tongue twisters. All you really need to know is that norepinephrine is a chemical found in both the central and peripheral nervous systems. It is the chemical responsible for happiness and the unleashing of all pleasurable emotions. If your diet lacks norepinephrine, you will quite literally not be able to fully enjoy life.

Once again the love addict is at risk. Some simply have a bad diet, or eat healthy meals only when with the beloved. The inconsistent norepinephrine means that the feelings of misery and depression when separated from the loved one are chemically enhanced by your own body.

What are the best sources of phenylalanine? These are simpler than the name—white meat of turkey, baked flounder, dry cottage cheese, and roasted peanuts. And as a bonus, if you are watching your weight, all these foods are natural appetite suppressors.

Niacinamide

Niacinamide is nature's tranquilizer. Since the serious consequences of chemical tranquillizer addiction became known, a number of researchers decided that taking pills for stress was wrong. Stress, they pointed out, is a natural aspect of life. Without it, life has no excitement, no adventure. After all, there is stress of a positive nature when you fall in love, when you have sex, when you get a job, a raise, or a promotion, and when you have other happy experiences.

There were numerous efforts to find ways to reduce stress without drugs. Among these were biofeedback, meditation, and similar mental approaches. In addition, there were nutritional studies to see whether, by changing your diet, you could find a way to calm an excess of physical and emotional stress. Eventually the answer was found in the form of the B-complex vitamins, most specifically vitamin B-3.

Vitamin B-3 is found in two forms. Niacin is the most common but has an embarrassing side effect: take more than 50 milligrams and you are likely to flush for a few moments. That is why most people using vitamin B-3 for stress purchase niacinamide. This is the same thing as far as your body is concerned, but you can take massive doses without flushing.

If you're not getting niacinamide in your diet, either from food or through a supplement, you'll have a hard time handling stress. The lack of it, in fact, prevents you from having rational thought. When mescaline was studied to learn why it caused a user to hallucinate, it was discovered to rob the brain of niacinamide. In fact, the antidotes for almost every hallucinogen are massive doses of one or more of the B-complex vitamins.

Some people have the mistaken idea that the removal of niacinamide from the diet is the way to handle stress. They think this will be a natural way to escape life, to go on a "trip," hallucinating without extra chemistry and somehow "relaxing." The problem is that an absence of niacinamide, like the use of hallucinogenics, creates an unpredictable condition that will vary with the same person. At one time you might feel yourself happily floating with the clouds, warmed by the sun, watching shimmering color changes as you float over fields of wildflowers. The next time, doing nothing different to create the "trip," you might believe that you are being pursued by a fire-breathing monster. Instead of peace, you find abject terror, unable to distinguish between reality and fantasy.

The way to handle stress with niacinamide is by taking a quantity of the vitamin researchers have found effective: 3,000 milligrams (3 grams), ideally in conjunction with from 500 to 1,500 milligrams of pantothenic acid, another B-complex vitamin.

This large quantity is not taken all the time—only when you feel that the stress is out of control, perhaps combined with extreme muscle tension. The combination of niacinamide and pantothenic acid is identical in effect to 5 milligrams of a minor tranquilizer from the benzodiazepine family, except with the adverse side effects of greater stress and addiction. And as with all B-complex vitamins, if you have taken too much, you will pass it harmlessly with your urine.

You will need to buy niacinamide in supplement form when you feel the need for a natural tranquilizer. However, you can aid your body by obtaining a smaller quantity through the regular consumption of bran. It is also found in yeast, as is pantothenic acid.

Other Useful Vitamins

Magnesium deficiency can be another concern. It causes apathy, belligerence, and/or a sense of withdrawing from others. Vitamin B-6 deficiency leads to irritability, an inability to concentrate, nervousness, and headache, all symptoms that can be mistaken for those of a love life problem. And general emotional problems may be helped by focusing on vitamin C, phosphorous, and the B-complex vitamins.

Among the best foods to incorporate regularly into your diet are fresh or fresh-frozen fruits and vegetables (without added sugar); organ meats; whole grains; egg yolks, meat, fish, and poultry; green leafy vegetables; milk and milk products; baked potato (with the skin, which contains most of the nutrients); wheat germ (if you like breakfast cereal, instead of the processed products try buying inexpensive packages of whole puffed wheat, complete with the wheat germ. No sugar is added and the taste is excellent); green peppers, citrus fruits, tomatoes, broccoli, and strawberries; sardines, herring, and salmon; peanuts and walnuts (walnuts also lower cholesterol, as can vitamin C); and rice bran.

There are others as well, but this list should make it clear that a good diet is also an enjoyable diet. And a good diet will assure that your recovery is swift. You will not find yourself mistaking the depression of improper body chemistry with the depression caused by failure to heal your love addiction.

Nutrition and Sex

Some love addicts claim that their sex drive is not so strong after they have stopped obsessively pursuing their beloved. Earlier we discussed the physiology of sex, but there are two additional nutritional factors of which you should be aware.

The normal sex drive for an adult is now believed to be what you experience around the age of thirty. There should be no radical decline for men or women after this period, although each may seem to peak at a different age. This means that if you are capable of enjoying sex five times a week at the age of thirty, you will be able to pursue at least that frequency into old age.

Many factors can contribute to a decline in your sex drive, including side effects to some medications. However, in my research I have found that there are two problems for most love addicts. First, they tend to have a high sugar diet until they have completely worked this program. This increases the need for B-complex vitamins, the absence of which causes a decrease in the sex drive. "Sugar junkies" make lousy lovers, but this is an easily corrected problem.

The second problem comes from drinking caffeinated beverages—coffee, colas, and the like. The dangers or lack of dangers from caffeine are no longer so certain as they once were. Depending upon the quantity you consume during the day, there may even be some benefits. But the one fact that has been clearly demonstrated and established is that drinking caffeine fairly close to going to bed diminishes the sex drive. Stay with decaffeinated drinks before making love, enjoying caffeine, if you must, when you are not going to be intimate. Assuming you are otherwise in good health, that change alone will eliminate yet another problem you might have previously blamed on your love addiction.

Step 3: Exercise

I hate to mention exercise. It is one of those terms that seem to evoke an intense (and sometimes very hostile) response. For some people, the thought of exercise is about as welcome as the clanging bell of the ice cream truck—to the parent who has managed to get several overactive children to lie down for their nap. To others it carries all the joy of winning the Publisher's Clearing House Sweepstakes.

Exercise is anything you do that improves your cardiovascular system and helps you metabolize your food. One form of exercise is the typing needed to write this book. In fact, several years ago, when manual typewriters were just beginning to be replaced by electric machines in most offices, the new technology was found to come with one bad side effect. Professional typists who spent most of the business day working a manual typewriter would gain an average of five pounds the first year following the switch to an electric. The lowered exertion rate with the electric typewriters was just enough to make the difference. The only way to counter this problem was to increase other forms of exercise.

Business travelers get a bit less exercise today than in the past because they fly instead of taking the train. Men and women traveling by train could walk back and forth through the cars, and frequently did. They certainly had to move about to eat, to smoke, and to go to the bathroom. And if they wished to do so, they could stroll back and forth among the cars while the train was in motion.

Air travel ended all possibility of exercise. Restrooms are close at hand, and meals are brought to you. The narrow aisles must be reserved for flight attendants and those going to the restrooms. It's not an enormous change, but frequent travelers of the past were slightly better exercised than frequent travelers of today.

Fortunately, these rather unpleasant, though unavoidable, realities have their positive sides. They show that it is also quite easy to get exercise, and that if you plan matters correctly, you can do it with a minimum of lifestyle change.

If you live in the city, even if you are avid about exercise and belong to a health club, read on. Photosynthesis is the one area where most urban dwellers are deficient, from those who consider exercise a matter of changing TV channels manually to those who regularly take time for a five-mile run on an indoor jogging track at the club.

Your first concern is obtaining full-spectrum light for at least twenty minutes a day, seven days a week. The simplest approach is to take a brisk walk during your lunch hour or at some time before it is dark. It doesn't matter if the day is overcast; you will benefit as long as there is daylight. Full-spectrum light is needed to create the natural form of vitamin D that acts as a tranquilizer. Supplemental vitamin D does not have the calmative properties of the form of the vitamin created by your own body.

If you have used work to escape from relationship problems much of the year, you have probably gone to work before full daylight and returned after dusk. You may also take your recreation indoors, watching television or going to an athletic club. This will lead to a degree of depression no matter what else you do.

There is an alternative to outdoor exposure, if necessary,

which is to use full-spectrum fluorescents either at work or at home. Such illumination is readily available in garden supply shops, because it is used for indoor gardening. Bulbs are not expensive, and fit in a standard desk lamp. They also last through years of use. They are frequently, used in parts of the north where winter means few daylight hours, and people develop emotional illness from the nearly endless darkness.

Other kinds of exercise can be added, depending upon your personality. Do you drive to work? Park your car farther away than usual, forcing yourself to add at least a half-mile walk in the morning and evening. If you take public transportation, get off one stop before or after your regular stop to assure a walk.

Can you use steps in your office building? Then do so. If you are on a high floor, try climbing the first two flights, then take the elevator the rest of the way, or take the elevator to a point two floors below your office and walk from there. If you can go more than two flights, do so. The point is to begin getting some exercise without feeling you are on a formal program.

If you visit other offices, repeat the parking and stair climbing approach whenever possible. One of my patients works in an area where parking is limited to the employee lot. She walks around the block once each time she has to go to or from the parking area. It is not much of a difference, but she has found that over time she has lost a little weight and firmed up her body, and she feels better about herself.

If you love pets and can realistically take care of a dog, this may be an answer for you. Dogs need to go outside several times a day for brief periods, and can also serve as both your excuse for and companion on a long walk every morning. Extremes of weather will not bother your dog, and the early morning will not be a problem regardless of the climate where you live.

An ideal approach is to spend the first five minutes encouraging the dog to "perform" at fire hydrants and trees. Then walk the dog as briskly as possible for twenty minutes or longer. The dog will adapt to walking instead of sniffing and marking each tree, if you encourage it to do so. And you both can use the exercise you might not otherwise get. Remember, however, that there is much more care involved with dogs than with, say, cats; don't get a dog just for exercise unless it will fit the way you are able to live.

Should you want to exercise with a group, choose a facility

that fits your needs. The health benefits and ease of working out are similar among gyms, Y's, and health spas; the main differences are in cost, age, and decor. Whatever you decide to do, at any rate, make certain you will keep it up. You may have a body that cries out for a daily workout at a health spa, but if you believe that humans were never meant to sweat and that "exercise" is a dirty word, don't join a club. You won't use it. Instead, do something simple, such as parking farther away from the office and store than usual. Even slight changes in your activity pattern will help.

Step 4: Psychological Reinforcement

Nutrition is important, but you may wish to use psychological reinforcement as well. It is important to be certain the subconscious mind is fully healed, and the following exercises can provide the extra help you may need.

There are a number of ways to obtain this reinforcement, but one of the most effective is an approach to psychology known as *psychosynthesis*. The idea behind this approach is that there is an aspect of the mind that knows everything, that can guide you along the right path, reinforcing your choice for a better life. Some therapists like to think of this aspect of the mind as a guru, a wise old being, perhaps a man, perhaps a woman, perhaps a wisdom that transcends a physical body. Other therapists talk of the Inner Self Helper, while those who are religious may look upon this part of the mind as a pathway to God. They say that it is the manner in which God talks with mortals—perhaps what is sometimes called the Holy Spirit.

Whatever it may be, and whatever you are comfortable calling it, the following exercise taps into the wisdom you are seeking.

Exercise 1: The Temple of Silence

Start with the fractional relaxation used in chapter 6. Then, once you are relaxed, visualize yourself standing at the foot of a high mountain on a beautiful day. If comfortable doing so, bring your beloved inner child with you. The two of you will wish to share this experience, because it will enhance your new unity. Either way, you experience the sun so warm that it seems to envelop you like a comforting blanket. The sky is a brilliant blue, with puffy white clouds lazily floating above. You can hear birds singing a melodious song so pleasant to your ear that you find yourself smiling happily. The air is crisp and clean, and you hear a brook running through a meadow, the water pure and delicious. There are wildflowers in bloom, creating what looks like a carpet of color more beautiful than the most expensive Oriental rug. You are completely at peace.

Look more closely at the mountain. Notice that there is a gently sloping path working its way upward. The path is naturally smooth and even, and walking it is no more difficult than walking along a city sidewalk or country lane. Even if you are out of shape. Even if you are overweight. Even if you are in some way physically disabled, you know that the path is one you can traverse with ease. The quality of the path, the beauty of the day, and the happiness you wish to enhance through greater knowledge all propel you forward.

You make your way to the top, and instead of being tired, you are even more refreshed. It is as though the radiance of the morning is enhanced by the greater altitude.

Ahead of you is a building, the Temple of Silence. It is a shelter as inviting as an oasis, as a cool drink on a hot day. There is nothing special about the design. It may be Oriental or ultra-modern. It may look as though it was built by one of the world's great architects, or it may look like a rough-hewn cabin built by a pioneer moving West. Whatever shape would be most inviting to you, that is the shape it takes.

Just before the temple is a clearing, where you pause to look around. You instinctively understand that the Temple of Silence is the sought-after end to many journeys concerning your past, your present, and your future. There are no secrets in the Temple of Silence. There is no need for secrecy. You know that, inside the temple, your heart can be laid bare. If you have acted in a manner you now find shameful, there is no recrimination. Your past is accepted, understood, with no need for forgiveness. And if you have made choices that were the right ones for yourself and your relationships, you feel an enhanced sense of success. You have taken steps from which you will never have to retreat. Either way, for what may be the first time in your life, you are safe from all the traumas of the world and the mind, and you walk inside the temple.

The temple is dark when you enter, except for a shaft of light so inviting you walk into its brightness. The light surrounds you like a second skin, your entire being becoming serene. For a moment you do nothing except experience the light, experience the peace. You are aware of the elevation of the temple at the top of the mountain. You feel emotionally expanded, the world pleasantly quiet and relaxed.

Your eyes have adjusted to the brightness and you see a staircase in the center of the beam of light. You walk toward it, knowing that all answers will come to you when you have reached the top.

The climb to the top makes your mind calm, open, and alert. At the highest point you find a large platform, on which you meet a wise being of all knowledge. This is the person you have been seeking, and you know immediately that all answers will be yours. There is a peace as great as when you were in the womb, yet you are also aware that the person is the source of the light, and you are filled with its radiance. Your body has become as one with its healing properties.

As you experience the light, you look into the eyes of the wise old being. You sense love in them, unconditional love, total acceptance for who you have been, who you are, and who you will be. Your clothing does not matter. Your job does not matter. Your bank account does not matter. All the artificial trappings of life by which we too frequently stand in judgment of others have no meaning to the wise being.

If you have brought your inner child with you, and I hope you have, because he or she is experiencing the same feelings and emotions as you are, then the three facets of your personality are all present together. First there is your inner child, the previous unfulfilled past with whom you have been lovingly reunited. Then there is yourself as you exist today. And with the two of you is the being who is actually your higher self. If you are a religious person, you might consider this to be your spiritual self.

The idea of three aspects to every human is not a new one. Carl Jung called these parts the "pyramid of humanity."

Now I want you to enter into an inner dialogue with the aspects of your pyramid of humanity. Introduce your inner child to your higher self, making a direct, complete connection between the two of them.

Take your time. Talk with your higher self. Discuss what has happened, what you have done to heal, how you feel, and what you plan for your future. Bring your inner child into the conversation, because the three of you will be working together to assure a better future. Let the dialogue roam wherever you desire. You don't have to involve your inner child with all the questions you may ask. It is enough for you to have made the introduction.

Once you are finished, have your inner child talk directly with your higher self. Let the inner child ask any questions he or she may have. Let your inner child share any special, personal feelings.

The conversation will not involve you at the moment, but feel free to listen in. You are not an intruder. You are welcome to hear everything. There are no secrets among you. All is well. All is good. You are experiencing the pain of the past with the understanding of your higher self, and together they are presenting you with the information you need to change your life.

Now your life will be going in the right direction. The era of your being a puppet of your past is over. The strings have been cut. The puppet has been transformed into a living, breathing, independent human being in control of his or her own life.

Exercise 2: Integration

Keep your eyes closed after you have finished the internal conversations. Be certain that all questions of the moment have been asked and answered. Then inhale deeply, exhale slowly, feel yourself peacefully relaxed, and start a new visualization.

This time I want you to visualize that precious, special trio—your inner child, the wise old being, and yourself as you are now. They are in front of you, holding one another, so happy to be together that they are integrating themselves, the three blending into one. Your hearts, your minds, and your bodies are melding together. For the first time, your inner child has lost his or her fear, sadness, and longing. Your higher being no longer aches to ease that pain because the wisdom of the higher being, the understanding, have all passed to the inner child. And with the two blending into you, there is peace, happiness, a rebirth without the sorrow of your love-addicted past.

The inner child is actually the physical embodiment of your childhood, painful as it was and brutal as it was. Your inner child has been tormented, filled with fear and rage, filled with a sense of helplessness and hopelessness. Now all of that becomes you, yet in so doing, the inner child gains your knowledge and wisdom. The inner child gains the hindsight of the adult, and emotional changes begin. Finally your higher self enters this blend. Any remaining confusion that exists is eliminated with the compassion, the awareness, and the cognizance of your higher self. Thus, as you blend together you feel peace, happiness, a healing passing through your body, your mind, and your spirit. You feel an inner glow, a warm sense of security and self-confidence.

Perhaps this will come instantly. Perhaps it will come over the next few hours, as you walk about, eat, sleep, work, or otherwise experience a normal day. The time for completeness does not matter. What is important is that the process has begun.

Exercise 3: Joy and Peace

Now, still keeping that image of the integrated self in front of you, visualize the rest of your body completely surrounded by warm, white light. Then pull the image of the integrating trio into yourself, making it one with you.

Next do the same thing visualizing the image of the integrating inner child, current self, and higher self to the left of your body, again, the rest of your body surrounded by the white light. Then repeat with the image on the right side of your body, always pulling it in. Follow with the image behind you, then the image above you, and finally with the image below you.

Each time this enters a different part of your body, try to feel the inner glow. Try to feel the sense of peace, harmony, integration, self-confidence, healing, and happiness. You may sense that you are physically lighter, for you have let go of your past, let go of your codependent behavior. All the trauma has been released. You are feeling yourself grounded in the here and now, and it is good. There is a growing sense of inner contentment filling your being.

Exercise 4: Affirmation

Once you have completed this journey, I want you to work on a series of exercises originally developed by John Bradshaw, author of the book *Homecoming*. I have attended many of his workshops, as have many other therapists. All have found that his techniques enhance the healing of love addiction described in this book. Bradshaw was also the first person to articulate the idea of the inner child, though the concept of our lives being dictated by the unresolved conflicts of childhood is not a new one. The child, as it has long been said, is parent to the adult.

Imagine or remember yourself as early as you can as a child. There is no best time to recall. Some people seem to remember themselves when they were in the crib or playpen. Others remember an important event, such as the discovery of their hands and feet, the first time they crawled or walked, a fifth birthday party, or the first day of elementary school. It does not matter how far back you go. Just try to remember the earliest time, whether as an infant, a toddler, or perhaps a seven- or eight-year-old. You might imagine the room where you were born. You might imagine yourself in the first grade.

I want you to see yourself as you were, handsome or beautiful, a delightful child, one you, as an adult, would instantly love if you encountered him or her today.

Now imagine that you can hold that small child, yourself when you were young. You might fantasize that you have the power of a wise and loving wizard who can at once be who you are yet return to the past to give love to who you had been.

Become, for a moment, that child and make yourself aware of the presence of yourself as an adult. The child does not realize that is who you are, of course. All the child sees is a kindly adult, a gentle adult, a loving, accepting, good adult who brings a warm glow of love to the child's presence. The child (you) recognizes that the adult (you) can supply all the unfulfilled needs and wants that the child's parents are not providing.

Now let the child (you) experience the grown-up (you). Feel the grown-up's strong, loving arms. Let the child feel the comfort of being held, carried, sensing safety, sensing unconditional love.

Now, as your adult self, cradling your inner child, I want you to say the following affirmations developed by John Bradshaw:

"Welcome to the world. I've been waiting for you."

"I'm so glad you're here!"

"I've prepared a special place for you to live."

"I like you just the way you are."

"I will never, never, never leave you, no matter what!"

"Your needs are okay with me. I'll give you all the time you need to get your needs met."

"I'm so glad that you're a boy/girl" (depending upon which it is).

"I want to take care of you, and I'm prepared to do just that."

"I like feeding you, bathing you, and spending time with you, because I love you. I'll always love you, forever and ever."

"In all the world, there has never been another like you. God smiled when you were born."

Let yourself feel whatever you feel as you hear these affirmations. Hold your inner child close to you, assuring your inner child that you will never leave him or her. Assure your inner child that from now on you will always be available to him or her. Assure your inner child that, from now on, you will always love him or her.

Now become your grown-up self once again. Look down at your precious little inner child, and be aware that you have just reclaimed him or her. Feel that sense of reclamation, that homecoming; a feel that you *have* reclaimed that inner child, that you have become one together.

Now walk out of that room and out of that house, looking back as you stroll happily, confidently, down the integrated street of memories. You are an adult, but as you walk down the street, you can witness yourself at different ages, growing, learning, experiencing the life that preceded the life you now lead. From time to time you can stop and talk to the ever-older inner child you are passing.

Walk past your first elementary school and see your inner child attending classes.

Now repeat the affirmations you made to the younger inner child. "I'm so glad you're here. I love you just the way you are. I will never, never leave you, no matter what. Your needs are okay with me. I'll give you all the time you need to get your needs met. I'm so glad you're a boy/girl. I want to take care of you and I'm prepared to do just that. I like spending time with you. In all the whole world, there has never been another like you. I love you. I love you. I love you. I will never, ever leave you.

"And because I'm here, it all turned out all right. No matter how bad it was then, it all turned out all right.

"God smiled when you were born!"

Feel the sense once again of that reclamation, that homecoming.

Now continue walking up the road of memories to yourself as a teenager, and tell yourself, "I like you just the way you are. I accept you. I love you. Your needs are okay with me. I will never, never leave you no matter what. I'll give you all the time you need to get your needs met. I'm so glad you're a boy/girl. I want to take care of you and I'm prepared to do just that. I like spending time with you. In all the world there has never been a child like you. God smiled when you were born."

Assure your teenage self that you will never leave him or her, and that, from now on, you will always be available. Once more feel that wonderful sense of the homecoming, the reclamation.

When you have finished, inhale deeply, exhale slowly, then, relaxed, open your eyes.

Exercise 5: Write Your Feelings

Now I want you to write two letters. One will be from you to your inner child. The other will be from your inner child to you.

This exercise may seem odd at first, but it has been used by psychologists throughout the United States. It is a way of tapping your subconscious mind, or an aspect of your conscious being.

You will write the first letter with your dominant hand. Are you right-handed? Then use your right hand to write the letter to your inner child. Are you left-handed? Then your left hand will write to your inner child.

The first letter, your letter to your inner child, should be as emotional as possible. It should come from your heart, not your head. Remember the anguish that your inner child experienced over the years. Remember the pain, the loneliness, the longing and confusion. Just as you were in the previous exercise, you should be open and loving, revealing your heart, your caring, and your understanding. Try to think as your inner child might have been thinking over the years, and address him or her accordingly. Let the child know of your love, of your promise that you will never leave him or her, and of your understanding of his or her traumas. If you wish, you can tell your inner child how you are going to let the past be past.

Now switch your pen or pencil to the other hand, the hand you do not normally use for writing. Then, with a fresh piece of paper, have your inner child write a letter to you.

Do not try to make things easier by typing or using a computer. This is too personal for that, and the exercise will not work unless each of you can react individually.

Take all the time and all the paper you need. Do not worry about your grammar or spelling. Do not worry about restraining your emotions. If you are angry, express that anger. All the emotions that will be expressed are from within. They are from your inner child, and this letter is between you and your inner child. Every emotion you are feeling, no matter how good or bad you may view it, is from the past.

Some people are angry with their inner child. Some people love their inner child. Some people are sorry for their inner child.

Don't try to compare this exercise, and the personal letter you are writing, with the previous exercises. Yes, your inner child needed and needs your loving support. He or she is frightened, confused, filled with all kinds of emotions that you are only now healing, only now helping that inner child to handle. But because the inner child was not healed over the years, you experienced personal hell. You became a love slave, addicted to seeking relationships in which you relied upon others to meet your needs. Had you not had such pressures, your life would have been different. Thus, you may very well be angry at the actions of the inner child.

Remember that there is a difference between loving the inner child and being pleased with that inner child's actions. Through the naive viewpoint of his or her youth, your inner child may have caused you all kinds of problems that now greatly anger you. That is all right, and if that is what you need to tell your inner child, then do so in the letter you are writing.

Some people are afraid of their inner child. Some people are afraid to feel the pain of their inner child, because there *is* pain in there, I assure you. In more than twenty-five years practicing psychotherapy I have never met anyone who did not have at least some pain in childhood.

Your inner child may also be angry with you. Look how long you took to return, to greet that inner child, to help the inner child understand the love and nurturing of which you were capable.

Do not try to restrict your inner child's writing. You have given up control by holding the pen or pencil in the hand you normally do not use for writing. Let the inner child reveal himself or herself to you, perhaps responding to your letter, perhaps expressing himself or herself for the first time.

Again, take as long as you need. Do not hold yourself back.

I had a group of men and women, love addicts all, work this program, and their experiences were quite similar to what I think yours will be. They found that there was anger toward their inner child, and anger with their grown self by the inner child. They had lived lives of mutual misunderstanding and pain, all the time sharing a single body that others saw as strong, healthy, and without problems, except in relationships.

Typical of the letters that resulted from the exercise was the following. A woman wrote to her inner child, being both reassuring and letting the anger come forth. She wrote:

"You are a special, gifted, and beautiful child. Your smile lights up the world with its shine. It gives me great pleasure to see you, be with you, hold you. You bring joy to so many. You are really a gift from God. I love you. I have always loved you. I want to be with you always.

"If you want to achieve something, you can. I'll support you no matter what."

Then the woman's tone switched to anger and anguish. She continued her letter by saying, "Why weren't you there for me? I believed in you, but you left me and made me alone, made me feel like no one loved me, like no one could love me. I don't want to be alone, and I don't want to be a failure, and I feel like I can't succeed. Why do I always have to excel? Why can't I win? Why can't I be loved? I have so much to give, to share, and I can't give enough. I want it all. Is it possible? Yes or no?"

Then she switched the pen to her other hand and let the inner child respond. At first she was supportive, but then the plaintive cry of long-time anguish was heard. The inner child wrote,

"It's possible [to have it all—love, happiness, personal success]. You just have to believe and trust. If you trust in yourself, you can do it."

Then the inner child continued, "I don't believe in myself and I feel it's all your fault. Why weren't you there for me? Why didn't you love me enough?"

The understanding the woman gained reinforced the integration she achieved that session. She faced her pain, gained understanding, and learned to love. What had been an intensely difficult time for her became one of healing that led her into the world as a person who had triumphed over personal, internal hell.

The same will occur for you as you work this program, as you at last exorcise the personal demons that have been driving you through no fault of your own.

Why Love Yourself?

Why is it so important that your inner child feel wanted and loved, to know that he or she will never be alone again? Because when you can get that message through, you will break down the walls of your love addiction.

You are love-addicted to the extent that the little child, your inner child, doesn't believe it is loved. You are love-addicted to the extent that that little child is looking for the love it never had. You are love-addicted to the extent that that little child is waiting to be loved by people on the outside.

But people on the outside cannot love your inner child until *you* love that little child yourself. Only when you love yourself, only when you exude that self-love, will you also exude a positive self-image. And only when you exude a positive self-image can people love you.

This is not ego. This is not pride. This is being a whole person, moving into life as yourself, comfortable with your own existence, able to correct problems and accept your capabilities.

Someone who gives off a sense of self-hate or shows a lack of self-worth is not attractive to others. No healthy person is going to come over to you and inform you that he or she will do whatever it takes to make you happy. A healthy person wants to share a life, the good and the bad, the joys and the sorrows, always working together through life.

Love addicts come across as one of two kinds of personalities. They are either emotionally draining, people requiring so much reinforcement that there is no opportunity for interpersonal growth, or they are like mannequins. The latter allow for the projection of fantasy which, if fulfilled, must then be paid back by meeting the mannequin's needs. This is not conducive to a meaningful relationship.

You first have to have a positive self-image. You must believe in yourself, exude the self-confidence of loving and accepting yourself—not being desperately needy for love. Such desperation leads you right back into love-addicted relationships.

This is why your inner child must genuinely feel loved, wanted, and needed, and know he or she will never be alone again.

Some people come from the kind of religious background that stresses personal humility. They may worry that loving their inner child, believing in themselves as they are, loving themselves as they are, is somehow sinful. Perhaps self-love reveals a lack of true love for God, they seem to be thinking. Yet the truth is that if you believe in God and God's Creation, you must also believe in your own value. You were born as worthy as every person in God's Creation. Loving that which God was involved with making is loving that higher power in which you believe.

In effect, a deeply religious person is being disrespectful by failing to acknowledge his or her self-worth. The destructive aspect of the ego is in the love-addiction, not the healing. It is as though you are saying that God created junk, not someone of value.

No matter what your beliefs, happiness is your right. The pain of your childhood was wrong. The loneliness, the agony, the desperation that was caused by unfulfilled needs, all of that was wrong. Respecting yourself and demanding solid emotional health in a meaningful relationship is your right. More important, with the healing of your inner child, you will have stopped relying upon others for emotional stability and self-worth. You cannot walk hand in hand with your beloved until you can first walk alone. Healing your inner child assures that you can now take that walk, comfortable with yourself, able to seek a friendship, a meaningful romance, and long-term commitment. And the healed inner child results in the happiness that comes from healthy self love.

Exercise 6: Integrating Past and Present

The next exercise again begins with fractional relaxation. As you did before, go back to the period of early conflict in the family. This will usually be when you were small, perhaps seven or eight, and you first began feeling that your needs were not being met. Again, take a look at the inner child. See what the inner child is seeing. Explore his or her bedroom, and look at your parents as they were seen by your inner child. Make yourself as sensitive to all of them as you can. Then let yourself experience all of your inner child's unfulfilled needs. Make them a part of you so that you know the longings that needed to be met, yet never were.

Now go over to your inner child. You are both happy to see each other. Ignore your parents and put your arms around your inner child. Tell your inner child that he or she is loved, that you are big now and can protect your inner child in a way that no one did before. Then, with your arm comfortingly around your inner child, have your inner child tell your parents about the unfulfilled needs. Do not worry about the emotions of the experience. Your inner child may be crying or angry, timid or assertive. No matter what the situation, your loving support will enable your inner child successfully to say what must be said.

Now start to move forward in time, scanning all the relationships in which you tried to get your inner child's needs fulfilled.

Sometimes these were with neighborhood friends, school teachers, or other adults in your life. Sometimes these only occurred when you began dating. No matter what, you will find that seeking to have unfulfilled childhood needs met was a part of every intimate personal relationship.

Look at what happened with your first boyfriend or girlfriend, perhaps when you were in high school, perhaps when you were slightly younger or older, in college or on the job. Whatever your personal situation, start with that earliest relationship and examine each succeeding one in turn. Look at what you expected from those individuals. Look at the disappointments.

If you married unsuccessfully, or if you are currently in a disappointing marriage or other intimate relationship, examine the frustrations there as well. Think about all the childhood needs you wanted fulfilled yet that remain unfulfilled. You may have thought of these as failures on the part of the other person. You may have thought of these as failings within yourself. It does not matter who you blamed or who deserved the blame. Look at the unfulfilled needs of the relationship in light of the unfulfilled childhood needs you recognize in your inner child. Notice how each time you became involved with someone, you wanted that person to fulfill those needs that your parents failed to fulfill. In fact, you will probably find that some aspect of each person with whom you were involved reminded you of whichever parent most failed you.

A love slave usually discovers while doing this exercise that each lover was expected to behave as the parent failed to do. Yet no matter how the love object responded to you, it was never the right way, never good enough. This is because only your parents could meet your unfulfilled needs as a child. They did not do it then and they are not ever going to do it. The time for their involvement is over, whether they are living or dead. You have been letting your unfulfilled childhood needs dominate how you approached others, repeatedly dooming each new relationship to failure.

Now go back to childhood and talk with your mother and/or father, telling them how you feel about what happened to you. Don't try to hold back your emotions. You may be quite angry, and that is all right. Or you may find that your words are calm and reasoned, something you had not expected. You may find yourself speaking through tears. It does not matter. The important point is to tell them the truth.

For example, a woman might tell her father, "Do you remember when I dated Bill while in high school? I wanted him to meet the needs you never met when I was younger. I wanted him to show me the nurturing love you were always too busy with your work to give me. But he was just a kid who was interested in sports and going to the drive-in. He couldn't be you, and when he wasn't, I couldn't let myself keep dating him to see if he was right for me. I deliberately sabotaged our relationship in an effort to get your love.

"Then there was Jim at the office . . ." Again you tell what happened.

Each person—Larry or Sheila, Mary Ellen or Ahmad, Arnie or Naneesha—is discussed. You explain to your parent(s) how you effectively sabotaged the intimate portion of your life trying to get unfulfilled childhood needs met. In fact, you probably had one or more relationships with someone exactly like the parent who failed to meet your needs. And because the person was, in one or more important ways, exactly like the parent, your needs went continuously unmet.

Now, just as you did before, walk with your inner child into the present. Tell your inner child that you are going to meet your unfulfilled childhood needs. You are going to provide the love that was lacking. You are going to supply the nurturing support, the encouragement, the praise, and the respect that your inner child had every right to receive.

Tell your inner child that you recognize your parents will never meet the needs you had when small, and that you will do the loving from now on. Let your inner child acknowledge the comfort in this new, joyous relationship. Hold your inner child happily, sharing the new experience that is healing you both.

Never again will there be a need to have love for your inner child come from the outside. That love now comes from inside yourself. You are now in control, and together you and your inner child will accept that the past cannot be altered. Together you will seek only healthy, whole relationships with people on whom you will no longer project childhood needs and fantasies. You have confronted the parents who failed you. You have come to understand how you made so many mistakes over the years. And you have reached a point of change where you will be in charge of your own life, not a puppet of the past.

Once this is completed, once you and your inner child are together in the present, repeat the visualization exercise where you take your inner child into yourself, becoming one. Visualize the inner child in front, then in back, to each side, above and below yourself, each time drawing him or her into yourself. Feel how, with each taking-in of your inner child, you are filled with positive feelings. You are stronger, feeling sure of yourself and of a future where you can be in control—not a puppet of the past. You have fulfilled the unfulfilled childhood needs. You have given and are giving the love you failed to receive in a past that no longer matters. As you and your inner child repeatedly become one, you are strong, self-assured, and comfortable with the past because you have fulfilled what others neglected or ignored. You are able to accept the past, to feel good about the present, and to be in charge of your life as you move into the future.

Visualize New Possibilities

And now for a final exercise. Again, practice the fractional relaxation technique with your eyes closed. Now do a variation of the integration exercise where you became one with your current self, your inner child, and your higher self, pulling that image into your body.

This time you will use two different images. The first has to do with your work or whatever else is meaningful to you, apart from relationships. The other is a new relationship.

First, start with what you are realistically trying to achieve in your immediate future. This might be a new assignment for a freelance writer, a raise or promotion for someone who works in an office, or something similar. Visualize this and pull it into you from the front, back, sides, top, and bottom as you were shown.

For example, I started this book after teaching a course on ending love addiction. I had been working with love slaves through much of my practice, but always on an individual basis. I had taught people the methods in this book on a one-to-one basis and was not certain how much more I could do. However, when I was lecturing about the problem, I decided to try and go a step farther by having everyone work the program there in the classroom. To my delight, not only were they deeply moved, I heard from many of them later that the experience had been what they needed to begin their healing journey. Everything else was just a matter of reinforcement on their own time.

I decided that everything anyone needed to cure love addiction would go into this book. I wanted a reader sitting alone in a farmhouse in a small town in mid-America, a high-powered executive in a penthouse suite on Manhattan's exclusive Upper East Side, a cowboy on a ranch, a producer in a Beverly Hills mansion, a waitress in Seattle, and everyone else with love addiction to be healed. So I envisioned such people as my image. I saw these vastly diverse individuals, each with a different educational background, income level, race, and ethnic history, reading the book. All had tears of joy streaking down their cheeks as they were healed through the knowledge gained. And I also visualized myself doing the writing, remembering my patients and their healing, remembering what their needs were, what their questions had been, what their problems had been. I visualized myself writing for them, for the others, and for you, and all of you being able to heal yourselves from the affliction that has dominated your lives for far too long.

I also used verbal affirmations, another technique you can try. While doing the visualizing and drawing in to me, I was mentally saying, "I am writing effectively for my reader. My reader is enjoying this book. My reader is discovering the problems of the past and the healing methods of the present. My reader is finding peace and joy. My reader is ending her history of love addiction. My reader is finding happiness. And as my reader finishes my book, he is moving on to a new life—richer, fuller, and filled with joy in newfound, positive relationships."

The second image you will call up is that of you finding happiness with a new relationship. Don't put a face to this man or woman. Don't give him or her a name. You might do what some television news shows do when someone is speaking but must have his or her face disguised. You can picture yourself laughing, happy, emotionally and mentally stimulated, holding hands and talking with the person whose face is in shadows. You don't know what the person looks like in any way. There are no distinguishing marks, no indication of height or weight. You are just there together, and for the first time this is not a fantasy. You are healed and the object of your delight is also healed. You are coming together as mature adults, respecting one another for who you are, not who either fantasizes the other must be.

Your affirmation might be something like the following:

"I am finding happiness with a new man/woman. I am being

myself, liking myself, respecting myself. I occasionally make mistakes, but I correct them if possible and move on if I can't. That is what he/she likes about me. I am comfortable within, comfortable without. There are no illusions, no games.

"He/she is a whole person, happy and comfortable with him/herself. I have no illusions about this person, and I am happier than I ever could be when I was a love addict. My life is good. My life is rich. My life is fulfilling. And I come to him/her a whole person, receiving him/her as an equally whole person.

"This is the relationship I have dreamed about happening. This is real life, and it is good."

Will this work? There was a time when my own life was troubled from the past. My actions were nowhere near so extreme as those of some patients I have helped heal. Yet I did find myself working an early version of this program, which was still in development. The one part that was consistent was the affirmation you have just spoken.

Today I am happily married, committed for the long term, with a wife who I love and who loves me. Neither of us has a fantasy mate to be manipulated. We each accept the other person as is, being fulfilled by the reality instead of frustrated by an illusion. We each see the strengths and weaknesses in the other. We each experience aspects of the other that occasionally cause frustration. Yet from this union has come greater joy, greater happiness, and greater understanding than either of us thought possible. From this union has also come a son who is growing into independent manhood strong, self-confident without being self-centered, happy, warm, and loving.

That was why I started working in the field of love addiction. That was why I developed this program based on the best available research in psychology, as well as my own experiences with patients. That was why I decided to write this book, both to free you from your personal hell and to assure that you would not have to come to me or someone similar to get on the right track with your life. And that is why, if you have worked the program through to the end, you are now healed.

So write me in care of this publisher to tell me of your triumph. I want to know how you're doing. I care, and I'm delighted to know that, because of what you have read, your past is over and your present is a journey of happiness and fulfillment.

Appendix

The Program Recapped

The program for recovery from love addiction requires just eight steps, as you have seen. It has proven effective with thousands of individuals and has been adopted by many therapists around the country.

The eight steps are:

1. Determining whether you are a love addict by taking the self-evaluation test given in chapter 2.

2. Reviewing your relationship with your father as it relates to your present beliefs concerning your love object. This includes questioning the quality of life he enjoyed when pursuing his relationship(s) with women in the same manner that has left you miserable.

3. Reviewing your relationship with your mother, then considering her attitude toward how she was treated by your father. In both 2 and 3 you are working to think like your parent, though with an adult's understanding of what that means.

4. Reviewing the relationship between your father and mother. Often the love addict will structure his or her marriage or interpersonal relationship on the way his or her parents reacted to one another. If your parents were love addicts or otherwise codependent, then you may approach your relationships with the same attitudes and expectations. Once you know you are imitating your parents' relationship with each other, you can change.

5. Looking at your relationship through the eyes of your love object.

6. Coming to an acceptance of self as having personal worth and value. This is achieved through the fulfillment of childhood needs as accomplished in the earlier exercises.

7. Doing fractional relaxation and visualization exercises to reinforce the conscious decision to effect real change on a subconscious level.

8. Starting fresh with your love object, if the other person is emotionally healthy and wishes to try again, or moving on to the next relationship, one that will be constructive for all involved.

Bibliography

Alberti, Robert and Michael Emmons, *Your Perfect Right*. Impact Publishers: San Louis Obisbo, CA, 1986.

Assagioli, Roberto, MD, *The Act of Will*. Penguin Books: New York, 1976.

Assagioli, Roberto, M.D., *Psychosynthesis, A Manual of Principles and Techniques*. Penguin: New York, 1976.

Armstrong, Thomas, *The Radiant Child*. Theosophical Pub.: Wheaton, IL, 1985.

Bach, Richard, *The Bridge Across Forever*. William Morrow & Co.: New York, 1984.

Bandler, Richard and John Grinder, *Frogs Into Princes*. Real People Press: Moab, UT, 1982.

Bateson, Gregory, *Mind and Nature: A Necessary Unit*. Bantam: New York, 1988.

Beattie, Melody, *Codependent No More*. Harper/Hazelden: New York, 1987.

Benson, Herbert, *The Relaxation Response*. William Morrow & Co.: New York, 1976.

Botwin, Carol, *Men Who Can't Be Faithful*. Warner: New York, 1989.

Bradshaw, John, *Homecoming: Reclaiming and Championing Your Inner Child*. Bantam: New York, 1990.

Bradshaw, John, *The Family*. Health Communications: Deerfield Beach, FL, 1988.

Bradshaw, John, *Creative Love—The Next Great Stage of Growth*. Bantam: New York, 1992.

Branden, Nathaniel, *Psychology of Romantic Love*. Bantam: New York, 1980.

Buscaglia, Leo, *Loving Each Other.* Fawcett: New York, 1984.

Campbell, Joseph, *The Hero with a Thousand Faces*. Princeton University Press: Princeton, NJ, 1968.

Capra, Fritjof, *The Tao of Physics*. Bantam: New York, 1984.

Carnes, Patrick, *Sexual Addiction*. Comp-Care Publications: Minneapolis, MN, 1983.

Connell, O'Brien and Melvyn Kinder, *Smart Women, Foolish Choices*. Penguin: New York, 1986.

Cousins, Norman, *Human Options*. Norton: New York, 1981.

Davis, Adelle, *Let's Get Well*. Harcourt, Brace, Jovanovich: New York, 1965.

Dowling, Colette, *The Cinderella Complex: Woman's Hidden Fear of Independence*. Pocket Books: New York, 1981.

Duras, Marguerite, *The Lover.* Harper: New York, 1985.

Durrell, Lawrence, *The Alexandria Quartet: Justine, Balthazar, Mount Olive, Clea*. Penguin: New York, 1991.

Dyer, Wayne, *Your Erroneous Zones*. Funk & Wagnall: New York, 1976.

Fitzgerald, F. Scott, *Tender Is the Night*. Collier, Withers, Macmillan: New York, 1933.

Forward, Susan, *Toxic Parents*. Bantam Books: New York, 1989.

Forward, Susan and Joan Torres, *Men Who Hate Women and the Women Who Love Them*. Bantam: New York, 1986.

Fraiberg, Selma H., *The Magic Years*. Charles Scribner & Sons: New York, 1959.

Freud, Sigmund, *Totem and Taboo*. Vintage Books/Random House: New York, 1918.

Fromm, Erich, *The Heart of Man*. Harper & Row: New York, 1964.

Fromm, Erich, P.T. Suzuki, and Richard DeMartino, *Zen Buddhism and Psychoanalysis*. Harper Colophon Books: New York, 1960.

Gardner, John W., *Self Renewal*. Harper Colophon Books: New York, 1963.

Gawain, Shakti, *Creative Visualization*. New World Library: San Rafael, CA, 1978.

Gibran, Kahlil, *The Prophet*. Random House: New York, 1951.

Goleman, Daniel, *Vital Lives, Simple Truths*. Simon & Schuster: New York, 1985.

Green, Bernard, *Goodbye Blues*. McGraw-Hill: New York, 1981.

Green, Bernard, *Your Child Is Bright, Make the Most of It*. St. Martin's Press: New York, 1982.

Green, Bernard, *Getting Over Getting High*. William Morrow & Co.: New York, 1985.

Halpern, Howard M., *Cutting Loose: An Adult Guide to Coming to Terms with Your Parents*. Bantam Books: New York, 1978.

Hart, Josephine, *Damage*. Ivy Books/Ballantine: New York, 1991.

Hendrix, H., *Getting the Love You Want*. Henry Holt: New York, 1988.

Hesse, H., *Steppenwolf*. Holt, Reinhardt & Winston: New York, 1964.

Hoffman, Bob, *No One Is to Blame*. Science & Behavior: Palo Alto, CA, 1979.

Huxley, Aldous, *Brave New World*. Random House: New York, 1956.

Huxley, Aldous, *Brave New World Revisited*. Harper Brothers: New York, 1958.

James, William, *The Varieties of Religious Experience*. Longmans, Green & Co.: London, 1929.

Janporski, Gerald, *Goodbye to Guilt: Releasing Fear Through Forgiveness*. Bantam: New York, 1985.

Jung, Carl, *The Nature of the Psyche*. Princeton University Press: Princeton, 1969.

Jung, Carl, *Collected Works*. Princeton University Press: Princeton, 1985.

Koestler, Arthur, *The Ghost in the Machine*. MacMillan: New York, 1978.

Khan, Hazart Inayat, *Spiritual Dimensions of Psychology*. Sufi Order Publications: Lebanon Springs, NY, 1982.

Khan, Pir Vilayat Inayat, *Introducing Spiritual Into Counseling and Therapy*. Omega Press: Santa Fe, CA, 1982.

Khan, Pir Vilayat Inayat, *The Message In Our Time*. Harper & Row: New York, 1979.

Keyes, Ken, Jr., *The Hundreth Monkey*. Vision Books: Oregon, CA, 1982.

Keyes, Ken, *The Handbook to Higher Consciousness*. The Living Love Center: Berkeley, CA, 1975.

Kiley, Dan, *The Peter Pan Syndrome*. Avon: New York, 1983.

Kushner, Harold, *When All You've Ever Wanted Isn't Enough*. G.K. Hall: Boston, 1987.

Laing, R.D., *Knots*. Random House: New York, 1970.

Laing, R.D., *The Divided Self*. Viking Penguin: New York, 1965.

Lawrence, D.H., *Lady Chatterly's Lover*. Penguin: New York, 1959.

Lawrence, D.H., *Women In Love*. Penguin: New York, 1920.

Lawrence, D.H., *The Lost Girl*. Penguin: New York, 1920.

Lawrence, D.H., *Sons and Lovers*. Penguin: New York, 1957.

Lilly, John C., M.D., *The Center of the Cyclone*. Julian Press: New York, 1972.

Maslow, A.H., *The Farther Reaches of Human Behavior* (2nd ed.). Viking Press: New York, 1971.

Maugham, Somerset, *Of Human Bondage*. Penguin: New York, 1978.

Maugham, Somerset, *Collected Short Stories*. Penguin: New York, 1977.

Miller, Alice, *The Drama of the Gifted Child*. Basic Books: New York, 1983.

Miller, Alice, *For Your Own Good*. Farrar, Straus & Giroux: New York, 1983.

Miller, Joy, *Addictive Relationships: Reclaiming Your Boundaries*. Health Communications: Deerfield Beach, FL, 1989.

Missildine, Hugh, *Your Inner Child of the Past*. Simon & Schuster: New York, 1963.

Moore-Lappé, Frances, *What to do After You Turn Off the TV*. Ballantine, New York, 1985.

Nabokov, Vladimir, *Lolita*. Vintage: New York, 1989.

Norwood, Robin, *Women Who Love Too Much*. Pocket Books: New York, 1986.

Ornstein, Robert and Paul Ehrlich, *New World, New Mind—Moving Towards Conscious Evolution*. Doubleday: New York, 1989.

Ornstein, Robert and Paul Ehrlich, *Multimind—A New Way of Looking at Human Behavior*. Houghton Mifflin: Boston, 1986.

Osheron, Samuel, *Finding Our Fathers*. Free Press: New York, 1986.

Oussianoff, Penelope, *Why Do I Think I'm Nothing Without a Man?* Bantam: New York, 1983.

Oz, Amos, *To Know a Woman*. Harcourt, Brace, Jovanovich: New York, 1991.

Peabody, Susan, *Addiction to Love: Overcoming Obsession and Dependency in Relationships*. Ten Speed Press: Berkeley, CA, 1989.

Peale, Stanton and Archie Brodsky, *Love and Addiction*. Signet: New York, 1976.

Pearce, Joseph Chilton, *The Crack in the Cosmic Egg*. Crown: New York, 1988.

Peck, Scott M., *The Road Less Traveled*. Touchstone/Simon & Schuster: New York, 1980.

Peele, Stanton with Archie Brodsky, *Love and Addiction*. New American Library: New York, 1976.

Reik, Theodor, *Of Love and Lust*. Farrar, Strauss, and Cudahy: New York, 1941.

Rogers, Carl, *On Becoming a Person*. Houghton Mifflin: Boston, 1961.

Rolfe, Randy Colton, *Adult Children Raising Children*. Health Communications, Inc.: Deerfield Beach, FL, 1990.

Russell, Bertrand, *The Conquest of Happiness*. Liveright: New York, 1930.

Russianoff, Penelope. *Why Do I Think I'm Nothing Without a Man*. Bantam: New York, 1983.

Sartre, J.P., *Psychology of Imagination*. Rider: London, 1950.

Schaeffer, Brenda, *Is It Love or Is It Addiction?—Falling Into Healthy Love*. Harper Collins: New York, 1987.

Shah, Indries, *Seeker After Truth*. Harper & Row: New York, 1982.

Shah, Indries, *The Sufis*. Doubleday: Garden City, NY, 1964.

Siegel, Bernie, *Love, Medicine, and Miracles*. Harper & Row: New York, 1988.

Slater, Philip, *The Pursuit of Loneliness*. Beacon Press: Boston, 1970.

Tanen, Deborah, Ph.D., *You Just Don't Understand*. Ballantine Books: New York, 1990.

Teilhad De Chardin, Pierre, *The Phenomenon of Man*. Harper & Row: New York, 1959.

Tennov, Dorothy, *Love and Limerence*. Stein & Day: New York, 1979.

Watts, Alan W., *The Way of Zen*. Random House: New York, 1974.

Woodman, Marion, *Addiction to Perfection*. Innercity Books: Toronto, 1982.

Whitfield, Charles, *Healing the Child Within*. Health Communications, Inc.: Deerfield Beach, FL, 1988.

Wickes, Frances, *The Inner World of Childhood.* Sego Press: Boston, 1988.

Wilber, Ken, *No Boundary.* New Science Library, Shambhala Publications: Boston, 1985.

Wilson, Colin, *The Outsider.* Buccaneer Books: Cutchogue, NY, 1990.

Woititz, Janet, *Struggle for Intimacy.* Health Communications: Deerfield Beach, FL.

Index